About Island Press

Island Press is the only nonprofit organization in the United States whose principal purpose is the publication of books on environmental issues and natural resource management. We provide solutions-oriented information to professionals, public officials, business and community leaders, and concerned citizens who are shaping responses to environmental problems.

Since 1984, Island Press has been the leading provider of timely and practical books that take a multidisciplinary approach to critical environmental concerns. Our growing list of titles reflects our commitment to bringing the best of an expanding body of literature to the environmental community throughout North America and the world.

Support for Island Press is provided by the Agua Fund, The Geraldine R. Dodge Foundation, Doris Duke Charitable Foundation, The Ford Foundation, The William and Flora Hewlett Foundation, The Joyce Foundation, Kendeda Sustainability Fund of the Tides Foundation, The Forrest & Frances Lattner Foundation, The Henry Luce Foundation, The John D. and Catherine T. MacArthur Foundation, The Marisla Foundation, The Andrew W. Mellon Foundation, Gordon and Betty Moore Foundation, The Curtis and Edith Munson Foundation, Oak Foundation, The Overbrook Foundation, The David and Lucile Packard Foundation, Wallace Global Fund, The Winslow Foundation, and other generous donors.

The opinions expressed in this book are those of the author(s) and do not necessarily reflect the views of these foundations.

Design
Charrettes
for Sustainable Communities

Design Charrettes
for Sustainable Communities

Patrick M. Condon

ISLANDPRESS

Washington • Covelo • London

Library of Congress Cataloging-in-Publication Data
Condon, Patrick M.
    Design charrettes for sustainable communities / Patrick M. Condon.
        p.   cm.
    Includes bibliographical references and index.
    ISBN 978-1-59726-052-7 (hardcover : alk. paper)—ISBN 978-1-59726-053-4 (pbk. : alk. paper)
    1. City planning. 2. Community development, Urban. 3. Sustainable development. I. Title.

HT166.C62135 2008
307.1'216—dc22

2007025913

Manufactured in the United States of America
10 9 8 7 6 5 4 3 2 1

To my grandchildren Toby Mallon and Reese Condon, and to all the other children of

their generation—a generation whose hopes rest profoundly with our own.

Table of Contents

View of a typical neighborhood in Vancouver, British Columbia. North American city districts built prior to 1950 were characterized by an interconnected and often highly regular street network organized around commercial streets that connected and served neighborhoods. Trips to destinations are always via the shortest practical route due to the short block length and the absence of dead-end streets.

Preface

Fly over any North American metropolitan region and look out the window. Two different cities lie below. The city built before 1950 is instantly recognizable. It's where the streets are in some form of grid or interconnected web, and where commercial buildings line the main arterial streets—the Broadways, the High Streets, and the Main Streets of towns. The size of the urban blocks (a *block* being any piece of land completely surrounded by streets) is almost universally about 4 acres of land in rectangles of roughly 600 x 300 feet. Inside each residential block there are usually dozens of individually owned rectangular parcels, sized between 1,500 and 6,000 square feet. Typically, each parcel has one building on it, usually, but not always, occupied by one family. If you look carefully enough, you can see separate entrances on some of these structures, signifying the existence of more than one dwelling in what must be a duplex, triplex, or fourplex structure.

As you look down, you can also see that a larger arterial street stands out from the otherwise uniform grid every six to ten blocks; you can see most of the larger commercial or institutional buildings strung along these streets. From the air, these commercial streets are visible as relatively pronounced threads in the generally uniform and continuous urban quilt of the city. It is the weave of the larger quilt that you see, not the separated pieces in it. Studying the scene carefully, you realize that these commercial streets are rarely more than a 10-minute walk from any home.

Still scanning this world from 10,000 feet, we see an unusual amount of activity at certain key crossroads in the grid. Commercial buildings line not just the arterial streets, but also spread to surrounding blocks. These areas of intense commercial use often take on the characteristics of a *downtown*, and indeed, when they are powerful enough and large enough, they *are* the downtown of the urban region below. Our focus sharpens as we concentrate on this impressive center, with its tall buildings and monumental civic structures. We may even become so fascinated that we fail to see

Downtowns are so impressive that we often lose sight of the fact that they are part of the same urban fabric as the older neighborhoods that surround them. In this view of downtown Chicago and its surrounds, we see a uniform block size that ably serves both skyscrapers and single-family homes.

that this downtown is simply a change in the intensity of the urban web, a place where the energies of the urban structure become more pronounced, but not unlike the fabric that surrounds it. The street and block pattern remains the same, linked to the larger landscape by hundreds of street connections, showing no distinction between where the downtown ends and where the rest of the city picks up.

If we can tear our eyes away from the downtown and take in the broader landscape again, sweeping in everything up to the distant horizon, we can understand this older city as a whole. It is a giant web of streets laid over whatever ecological structure supports it (river, ocean, port, elevated land, strategic site)—a structure that either gives way to the web or interrupts it temporarily, leaving a pattern of serendipity and compromise apparent from the air.

As the plane descends toward the airport, a different city comes into view, this one covering much more land. In this urban landscape, the interconnected web is gone. Taking its place is a system of highways and roads that is no longer weblike, but branching like a tree. In this newer landscape, the main trunks and leaders of the tree are the major interstate highways, and the larger branches are the limited-access parkways and state and provincial highways. From there you step down in scale to the wider surface arterials, which are frequently designed to accommodate eight lanes of traffic, with many more lanes at intersections to accommodate turns. The thinner branches decrease in scale from four-lane arterial, to two-lane arterial, to local collector street, to local road, to, at the very tips of the system, cul-de-sacs or dead-end streets. Here there are no blocks at all. Residential districts have withdrawn from the hubbub of the nearby arterial streets, protected by a maze of turns and dead-end streets designed to let you into and out of, but not across, the neighborhood. The residential buildings in these enclaves are almost universally occupied by single-family homes, frozen in this status by zoning bylaws that criminalize the sharing of structures with other families.

From the air you can clearly see the cars as they make their way down the branch tips from the cul-de-sacs, climbing the road hierarchy to residential road, collector, suburban arterial, major regional arterial, and finally limited-access freeway. All these cars must make their way to the same point on the "trunk" of this road tree, usually an on-ramp to the freeway. With every car in the whole vast landscape directed to this one point, congestion is inevitable. Yet one person's congestion is another person's opportunity. A road system that directs thousands of automobiles to one point makes a million-plus-square-foot shopping mall the only economically viable option for commerce.

View of a characteristic post-1950 neighborhood in Surrey, British Columbia. The area shown includes the same number of acres as in the view of the Vancouver neighborhood shown above. Arterials divide rather than join the districts. Houses turn their backs on the main streets. There are no commercial services, and most houses are on dead-end streets, forcing all trips onto arterials.

From up here, you can see that the mall or big-box center is not connected to anything in its community. An access road to the highway is its only connection to the outside world. In contrast to the older city, in which commercial activity was a thread binding the fabric of the city, here commercial activity is set off in isolation, connecting with the larger landscape only via the umbilicus of the access road and off-ramp.

If you have a keen eye, and if you become curious about these marked differences in city form, you will also notice how the separation that characterizes the commercial project is a feature of other types of projects too. Everything is separated: office parks, housing developments, even elementary schools are cut off from any kind of linkage to their community other than an access road.

The move away from the weblike universal street network to the treelike street hierarchy is just one aspect of our changing approach to city building, but it is a particularly important and metaphorically pertinent example. This book is a response to the perception, now very widespread, that we have lost much and gained little by choosing a city form characterized by the kind of radical separation of activities described above—by choosing to build a literally dis-integrated city.

This book is about design charrettes, a method that we as professionals, officials, citizens, and stakeholders can use to reknit the pieces of the city together for our children. It presents a proven process that we can use for getting all of the people presently responsible for building cities to collectively change the rules of the game. This book takes the view that the only way to create sustainable cities is to use integration and synergy as first principles for city design,

View of a suburb outside Washington, D.C. Each subdivision is its own discrete perfect jewel, as are the office, educational and commercial projects in the distance. Their only connection is via one access road that connects to a major arterial, which in turn connects only to the highway interchange. Congestion of the highway and the interchanges are inevitable in this schema.

and that the new city spread below us is demonstrably not in compliance. It is offered in the firm belief that the people who are presently engaged in the process of building this new city—its engineers, its architects, its planners, its regulators, and its activists—are the very same ones who have the competence, the power, and the desire to reknit this city so that it can be sustained. This is a self-help book for people who are dissatisfied by the dysfunctional cities they are creating and who want to change.

Acknowledgments

Many people have contributed to this work over the years. Literally thousands of people have participated in our charrettes and taught me the lessons that I try to convey herein. Naturally they are too numerous to mention, so I must limit it to the few. First I must acknowledge the pioneers who reinvigorated the use of charrettes in North America. The list includes the U.S. National Endowment for the Arts Design Arts Program, which sponsored a number of design charrettes in the 1980s. I am personally aware of the influence of the late Catherine Brown in that NEA effort and express my gratitude to her, as well as my regret for her untimely demise. Professor Douglas Kelbaugh, now dean and professor of architecture at the University of Michigan College of Architecture and Urban Planning, pioneered charrettes in his practice twenty-five years ago and was instrumental in helping us launch the Design Centre here in Vancouver. I am also grateful to the thousands of members of the Congress for the New Urbanism who typically use charrettes in their practice. Because of their collective dedication, charrettes are becoming part of the planning and development mainstream.

On a more personal note, I would like to also acknowledge my associates at the Regional Plan Association of New York, and in particular Mr. Robert Lane, their head of urban design, for what has been a particularly fruitful creative collaboration over the years. Many of the thoughts contained in this volume are the product of this collaboration. I would also like to acknowledge all of my colleagues at the

Design Centre for Sustainability at the University of British Columbia. I want to mention and thank Elisa Campbell, our director, and Ronald Kellet, my fellow senior researcher, in particular for enriching the charrette process well beyond what I have described. I must certainly also thank the University of British Columbia for supporting our work in various ways over the years and for applauding our somewhat unconventional attitude toward academic research.

Finally, a sincere acknowledgment to my family: my wife, Stacy Moriarty, for her support and participation in these efforts over the years and for her sharp and accurate insights; my children, Alanna, Ryan, Kate, and Will; and my grandchildren, Toby and Reese, to whom I dedicate this book.

Introduction

Design Charrettes

In a design charrette, participants are assigned a very complicated design project to complete in a very short time. The term *charrette* was coined at the end of the nineteenth century at the Ecole des Beaux-Arts in Paris. The architecture faculty of that school would issue problems that were so difficult few students could successfully complete them in the time allowed. As the deadline approached, a pushcart—or in French, a *charrette*—was pulled past the students' work spaces. Students would throw their drawings into the cart at various stages of completion, because to miss the cart meant an automatic grade of zero. We use the term in the same sense, only for us it also connotes working together in teams rather than individually. The charrettes we organize challenge participants to collaboratively solve what appears to be an impossible problem in what they may think is an absurdly short time. In this book we will try to explain why this works and why we think it's the best way to plan and design new and redeveloped sustainable communities. As defined in this book, *a design charrette is a time-limited, multiparty design event organized to generate a collaboratively produced plan for a sustainable community*. We hope that this book will help professionals, designers, advocates, planners, developers, and concerned citizens to create communities worthy of them and their children.

Who This Book Is For

This book is for people who urgently want to make our cities more sustainable. Many people feel this urgency. Citizens, local elected and appointed officials, and community stakeholders increasingly believe that our cities are unaffordable, too dependent on the automobile, require too many resources to build and maintain, and leave their residents emotionally and physically compromised. We at the Design Centre for Sustainability at the University of British Columbia, and the hundreds of people who have participated in the various initiatives of the Design Centre over the years, feel that there *is* a better way to design and plan new and retrofitted communities, and we have enough confidence in our approach to offer this recipe book for doing so—one neighborhood at a time.

Given the global scale of the challenges we face, climate change in particular, a "one at a time" focus on solutions at a neighborhood or district scale might seem too small. Certainly such huge problems require solutions at regional, national, and international scales. But global problems are generated at the neighborhood scale and should be solved there too. With 80 percent of North Americans now living in cities, it follows that our pattern of metropolitan living—how we heat and cool our buildings and how we move between those buildings—is the reason North Americans consume more energy per capita than anyone else on the planet.

At the Design Centre we have a maxim that expresses this point: *The site is to the region as the cell is to the body*. And just as the individual human cell has everything to do with the overall heath of the human body, the sustainability of the individual site, when replicated thousands of times in similar configurations, has everything to do with the overall sustainability of the region.

Such a self-evident assertion should go without saying, but most of the solutions proposed for fixing our cities focus not on site- and neighborhood-scale design, but on broader technological fixes (the hydrogen-powered car), policy changes (requiring the recycling of trash), or regional-scale initiatives (building a new transit line instead of a new freeway). This lack of perspective is so severe as to constitute a form of cultural myopia, particularly when it has long been known that residents of older, higher-density neighborhoods use their cars 40 percent less than residents of sprawl and therefore contribute 40 percent less greenhouse gas per capita.[1]

We know that the problems of our cities are severe, and we know that citizens care about them and would avoid sprawl if they had a choice,[2] but very little of this information and concern has been synthesized into a holistic understanding of what a practically achievable sustainable community might look like, or of how to assemble the policy tools to make it real. What's going on? Apparently, our ordinary problem-solving methods don't work when we are designing, planning, and building sustainable communities. At the same time we have improved our technical ability to create individual pieces of the metropolitan region—buildings, roads, airports, sanitary waste systems—we have also somehow produced urban regions that are much less than the sum of their parts. Most of the individual pieces of the metropolitan region work well—the shopping malls, subdivisions, office parks, and freeways—but taken together, they fail in crucial ways. Quite aside from the fairly universal sense that these landscapes are unattractive and difficult to revere, there is a more practical concern: the future cost of maintaining these urban landscapes poses a potentially crushing burden for our children. Each resident of a post–World War II residential landscape is responsible for about four times more road infrastructure than a resident of a pre–World War II landscape.[3] This figure does not even include the proportionally greater per capita provision of arterial roads, parking lots, and freeways typically found in these districts. Thus the per capita cost to maintain these landscapes is a perpetual tax liability for our progeny and could affect them just when oil costs are highest and the impracticality of total auto dependence becomes most obvious.

Our careful observation of these sprawling suburban landscapes suggests that they are a collection of impressive solutions to very narrowly defined problems—rational details adding up to an irrational whole. A suburban intersection, with its eight turning lanes and eight travel lanes, beautifully manages the turning demands of thousands of cars a day, but walking from one side of the street to the other seems to fall largely outside of the problem as defined. A gated housing complex can be an impressive and beautiful place to come home to, but the gate and wall mean that the community inside can never integrate with its surroundings. A protected riparian space can often provide critical habitat, but when it is hidden behind the Wal-Mart parking lot, its ability to uplift the lives of those who inhabit the district is severely limited. A well-designed and well-landscaped office park can provide an economic boon to the community, but when flung off into the undifferentiated landscape of suburban sprawl, it is impossible to serve by transit. All of these elements, however exquisitely designed they may be, do not add up to a whole worthy of the word *community*. The public realm of walkable streets, integrated natural areas, a network of parks, and freely accessible civic space is entirely missing from this landscape—traded in for eight-lane arterials and gated cul-de-sacs.

In short, it seems that as we increase our ability to break the problems of city building down into tiny elements—the subdivision, the shopping mall, the intersection, the protected open space—we decrease our capacity to integrate these elements around the connective tissue of a functioning public realm. The post–World War II urban landscape exhibits a dis-integration of its parts unknown in previous decades. The problem is not that we lack the knowledge to make good park systems, transportation systems, housing developments, shopping centers, and job sites; we have never been more skilled at those tasks. Our problem is that we no longer know how to synthesize those elements into a functioning and efficient whole. We don't need more detailed work on this or that element of the landscape to make it sustainable. What we need is a way to reassemble the pieces into a whole, into something worthy of the name *community*. The design charrette provides that way.

A Self-Help Book for Cities

Participants in our charrettes come from varied professional and personal backgrounds. Consequently, we always try to talk in a language that is understandable to all, even if it's their first exposure to city design. We have attempted to write this book in this same language to make it understandable by the average citizen, but also useful for the professional planner, architect, or engineer. We have used what might seem to be an unusual model to achieve this goal: the self-help book. We have noticed that self-help books, usually devoted to solving emotional difficulties, all seem to follow the same formula: First they state the problem. Then they describe the theoretical foundation for the book in accessible terms. Next they break the subject down into memorable elements (as, for example, in *The Seven Habits of Highly Effective People*[4]) and focus attention on each one in turn. This discussion is often followed by case studies and examples drawn from the author's real-life experience. We use the same format. Now that we've stated our problem—the dis-integration of cities—we will turn in the next chapter to the theory behind our proposed solution—design charrettes.

1. Charrette Theory for People in a Hurry

Sustainability: An Imprecise but Useful Concept

The word *sustainability* brings essential social, ecological, and economic objectives together into one imperative. In the real world, the social, ecological, and economic realms interact with one another in complex and unpredictable ways. The charrette method can accept this multitude of often conflicting objectives without becoming paralyzed by complexity.

Sustainability, as a term, defies precise definition: it is open-ended. Similarly important and powerful terms, such as *justice*, *patriotism*, *freedom*, *truth*, *beauty*, *God*, and *faith*, also resist clear definition in direct proportion to their power to inspire. The names of concepts that defy simple definition are often the words that most powerfully motivate individuals and cultures.

This is not to say, however, that attempts to define such concepts have not been frequent and wide-ranging. Sustainability is no exception. The most widely accepted definition of *sustainability* comes from the 1987 report of the World Commission on Environment and Development (also known as the Brundtland Report), which defined "sustainable development" as "development that meets the needs of the present without compromising the ability of future generations to meet their own needs."[1]

This elegant formulation conceals a number of complexities. The most fundamental of these reside in an implied limit on planetary resources and in the possibility that the flow of nature's services could become unbalanced. In short, an ecological view of the physical planet underlies the sustainability paradigm. This view contradicts the still prevailing schools of economic development theory that see the earth and its resources as without absolute limits.

From Watchlike Precision to Messy Complexity

Most credit the work of mid-twentieth-century naturalists and scientists such as Aldo Leopold (1887–1948), Sir Arthur Tansley (1871–1955), and Eugene Odum (1913–2002) for helping to initiate the shift to an ecological worldview. Those who hold to that view focus on the interrelatedness of animate and inanimate systems and on the subtlety of the nutrient exchanges that sustain them. Ecological thinking represented a departure from the still influential mechanistic model of cosmic order. Isaac Newton (1643–1727) and his followers imagined the universe as akin to a great watch, a mechanism of immense precision that responds predictably to causative forces. This assumption still dominates the majority of academic research efforts and underlies the assumptions of most of our planning and design disciplines.

From an ecological perspective, the world is not that simple. The gears in Newton's cosmic watch never changed shape and size in response to energy and nutrient flows. The watch itself never morphed into a larger, faster, more diverse, more complex machine over time in response to those flows, nor did entire functions disappear to be replaced by apparently unrelated functions. But such transformations are observable everywhere in nature at a level of subtlety and complexity that transcends simple mechanics.

Humans Make It Even More Complex

Brundtland's definition of sustainability contains a second complication: humans. The ecological worldview, as groundbreaking as it was, seldom seems comfortable including humans inside its framework. Equipped with either a strictly biological or a romantic view of nature, many ecologists have perceived human settlement as an impediment to ecological integrity. Forward-looking thinkers have acknowledged that this view is unnecessary and unproductive. John Lyle, for example, challenges the belief that human activities always require "mitigation" when they affect the natural landscape: "Rather than mitigating impacts, we might create ecologically harmonious development that by its very nature requires no mitigation, recognizing that humans are integrally part of the environment."[2] Green architect and sustainable development proponent William McDonough believes that "sustainable development is the conception and realization of environmentally sensitive and responsive expression as part of the evolving ecological matrix."[3]

In this way, then, human activities can lead to an increase in sustainability. This is a new and powerful idea, but it complicates matters. Although many components of the global machine can change their form or function as a response to changing energy and nutrient flows, humans seem unique in their ability to understand these flows and change them for the better—that is, with the intent of benefiting both the human community and the long-term health of the ecosystems that sustain it.

As if the addition of a conscious party, humans, were not complication enough, the definition of sustainability adds one even more daunting complexity: time. Brundtland's definition of sustainability includes an intergenerational responsibility. The long-term multigenerational effects of any decision must be considered before immediate needs are met. Coming up with solutions for *immediate* urban design problems that consider both humans and the long-term health of their environment can be a daunting enough task, but adding an intergenerational responsibility threatens to make such problem solving almost impossible. How can we deal, in our complex and multilayered democracies, with such challenges? Democratic public process models are needed wherein citizens can both understand these complex relationships and create ways to capitalize on them in their communities.

We Are Handcuffed by Our Methods

Our largely linear and mechanistic methods for solving local and even global problems seem ill suited to the task. For example, opposing camps of scientists are now debating the extent to which human activity is contributing to climate change. Both sides come armed with complex, sophisticated climate models. These models attempt to capture the "mechanics" of climate, assuming that climate is describable in mechanical terms. Newton lives on in these computer models, whatever their complexity. But the results remain inconclusive. Meanwhile, political leaders and those they represent still demand scientifically verifiable "proof" before they are willing to contemplate any new restrictions on the economy—proof that climate models can never supply, at least not before Greenland melts and the oceans expire.

John Lyle makes this point more simply: "The question is often asked: How much of this pollutant or that activity can the environment absorb before it becomes unacceptably damaging or life-threatening? This is like asking how many times one can beat a person over the head before he will die. . . . This is difficult to answer with any accuracy and usually not the most useful question anyway."[4]

Methods That Fail Globally Fail More Spectacularly Locally

This same mechanistic thinking is observable at the municipal scale. The Pruitt Igoe housing complex in St. Louis, Missouri, built in the 1950s and abandoned in the early 1970s, is but one tragic example of this methodological failure.[5] The Pruitt

French architect Charles-Edouard Jeanneret (pseud: Le Corbusier, 1887–1965) examines the model for his imagined "Radiant City." Conceived in the 1920s, it would not be until the end of World War II that actual projects like this were built. In the United States, this kind of project was often used to house poor families displaced when their traditional neighborhoods were cleared for urban renewal or highway building projects.

Igoe housing complex was designed to conform to French architectural theorist Le Corbusier's elegant but narrow formulation for a modern urban utopia. Provide enough air and light for all citizens, he said, and all will be well. His formulation excluded other cultural, social, and behavioral influences. He missed, or chose to ignore, the intimacy of connection between people, buildings, and streets that Jane Jacobs so famously described in *The Death and Life of Great American Cities*.[6] As a consequence, the project soon became uninhabitable and derelict.

Even more tragically, at the same time Pruitt Igoe was going up, many of St. Louis's most efficient and walkable neighborhoods were being torn down—all to make way for highways to farmlands that were soon to be suburbs. Each of these projects was a "rational" solution to a narrowly defined problem—one a solution to deal with a "housing" problem, and the other to deal with a "transportation" problem. The planners for each of these projects, probably quite brilliant within their

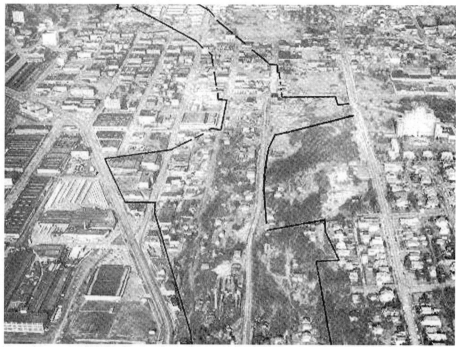

Aerial photograph showing the nearly completed clearing of inner-city lands for the construction of Interstate 70 in St. Louis, Missouri. Wide swaths of older inner-city neighborhoods
were cleared during the highway building boom of the 1950s, 1960s, and 1970s. Among the
consequences: divided neighborhoods in inner-city areas and easy access to the center city by
car from the surrounding countryside.

own defined disciplines, did not (or could not) consider the connection between
their two projects. Their linear methods and narrow problem definitions made it
impossible to see that connection.

These failures in St. Louis were failures of method. The narrow and mechanistic
methods chosen, so effective for getting men on the moon and exploding atomic
bombs, proved surprisingly ineffective for solving the smaller but more nuanced
problems facing urban North America. To solve such layered and complex sustainability problems, a more inclusive method is required. A design charrette is nothing
if not inclusive. A design charrette can handle both the physically quantifiable elements of the problem *and* those that cannot be quantified.

Working with this much complexity comes at a cost: in the face of so many
variables, we can never be certain that we have found the perfect solution. Perfect
solutions, in the sense that scientific methods require, are possible only for very

The Pruitt Igoe housing project was demolished by the St. Louis Housing Authority in 1972, after only twenty years of occupation. Despite conforming to Le Corbusier's principles, providing light, air, and green for every resident, it proved uninhabitable. Jane Jacobs and others took Le Corbusier to task for ignoring the organic relationship between people and the cities they inhabit, embodied in the urban syntax of street, stoop, entry, and parlor. None of these features are part of the Radiant City vision.

narrowly defined problems containing a limited number of variables. Any method for creating and implementing sustainable urban designs must accept all relevant variables from all three realms—social, ecological, and economic. We believe that the sustainable urban design charrette method meets this criterion. We further believe that sustainability problems, by their very nature, demand an inclusive and synthetic problem-solving process—precisely because they are divergent problems of the kind discussed below.

Sustainability Is a Divergent Problem, Not a Convergent Problem
Although they have phrased it differently, various philosophers, from Aristotle to Merleau-Ponty, have discussed the existence of two different kinds of problems: the convergent and the divergent. E. F. Schumacher, the British economist famous for his 1973 book *Small Is Beautiful*,[7] describes these concepts in an accessible and succinct way in his 1977 book *A Guide for the Perplexed*. As he put it, convergent problems tend toward a single and perfect solution: the problem is described, evidence is collected, and the problem is solved. He uses the invention of the bicycle as his example, suggesting that it provides an elegant solution for the problem of "how to make a two-wheeled man-powered means of transportation."

Schumacher suggests, however, that many other problems are more complicated. For example, "the human problem of how to educate our children" has two apparently supportable but opposing solutions. One solution would have us provide an atmosphere of discipline sufficient for experts to transfer information to children. If we are actively seeking the perfect solution implicit in any convergent problem, we might conclude that the perfect school would be one characterized by perfect discipline—that is, a prison. On the other hand, equally persuasive are those who find, on the basis of good evidence, that children respond best to freedom and find their own way to knowledge. In this case, the perfect school would be one that is characterized by perfect freedom—that is, "a kind of lunatic asylum." How, asks Schumacher, are we to resolve this contradiction?

There is no solution. And yet some educators are better than others. How does this come about? One way to find out is to ask them. If we explained to them our philosophical difficulties, they might show signs of irritation with this intellectual approach. "Look here," they might say, "all this is far too clever for me. The point is: You must *love* the little horrors." Love, empathy, *participation mystique*, understating, compassion—these are faculties of a *higher order* than those required for the implementation of any policy of discipline or of freedom. To mobilize these higher faculties or forces, to have them available not simply as occasional impulses but permanently, requires a high level of self-awareness, and that is what makes a great educator.[8]

Charrettes Provide a Method for Solving Divergent Sustainability Problems
Charrettes can help solve divergent sustainability problems. To be worthy of the name, a design charrette must elevate the contradictions inherent in the divergent questions confronted in our drive toward a more sustainable city to a level higher than "logic" or "proof"—it must create an atmosphere in which contradictions can be resolved not by proofs, but by empathy, intuition, understanding, and compassion. Elevating and resolving these contradictions through the agency of empathy, understanding, and compassion is not something you do alone. You do this with others.

The goal of any sustainable urban design charrette is thus to produce a design that embodies the higher-level empathy, understanding, intuition, and compassion of the design team in the form of a sustainable and implementable urban design plan. This is not to say that the resulting plans will perform poorly against measurable performance benchmarks, against traditional "proofs." On the contrary, we suggest that holistic, sustainable design solutions are best produced in an open-ended atmosphere in which empathy, understanding, intuition, and compassion can emerge. Such a broadly influenced design is unlikely to be perfect, but will probably perform better against a broad range of metrics than would a design produced by a small group of technical experts working within a narrow project scope.

The Design *Part of the Charrette*
Design charrettes are not planning exercises. *Design* is a key word worthy of additional attention. Since sustainability problems are, by definition, the manifestation of how social, ecological, and economic variables interact, the method used to *solve* sustainability problems must *acknowledge and manipulate* these interactions with the intention of producing a more sustainable city. Design as method meets these criteria.

Where linear methods become paralyzed in the face of multiple variables, design is comfortable. Even simple design problems have many variables and an infinite number of potential outcomes (modernist form-follows-function mythology notwithstanding—see the seminal work of Colquhoun to understand how this mythology operates[9]). Designers must accept the seemingly impossible challenge of determining every aspect of a physical space. Design cannot be "perfect" in all respects. An exceptional design is that design which comes closest to a perfect answer in a form that transcends the problem, raising it to a higher level through empathy, understanding, and compassion.

We often imagine the author of such a transcendent solution as a solitary genius. The truth is more complex. Increasingly, design is a collaborative activity, performed in teams. Everyone on the design team is a designer, including those without design training or experience. Design charrettes make citizens with a stake in their community (*stakeholders* is the inelegant but descriptive term) members of the design team. Their own empathy, understanding, and compassion fuel the creative collaborative process and allow the group to transcend the status quo.

The Charrette *Part of the Design*

Citizen stakeholders and public officials must dominate sustainable community design charrettes. Every identifiable group that has a stake in making the city more livable for current and future generations must participate in providing sustainable solutions for that city. All of us are familiar, however, with public consultation processes that similarly involve stakeholder groups, but break down under the weight of endless controversy. In this more usual circumstance, the elected officials in the community make their decision amid conflict, choosing the narrow interests of one side over the narrow interests of the others. Such a system does not resolve conflict, but rather institutionalizes it. Such a system cannot provide transcendent solutions grounded in empathy, understanding, or compassion, but only status quo responses—responses that, at best, produce dis-integrative "split-the-difference" solutions or, at worst, beggar one side of the conflict to the benefit of the others.

Design charrettes have become increasingly popular in North America as a means to overcome these problems. The U.S. National Endowment for the Arts Design Arts Program sponsored a number of design charrettes in the late 1980s and early 1990s. The NEA also sponsored the Mayors' Institute on City Design, which provided charrette-like collaborative sessions between mayors and design facilitators. Also seminal has been the work of many members of the Congress for the New Urbanism, whose members use the charrette method with community and private clients routinely and have done so since before 1990.

A design charrette changes the chemistry of the public review process. Stakeholders no longer have the luxury of maintaining their own narrow position from one meeting to the next without challenge. A charrette brings together stakeholderswho may have held dramatically opposed positions in the past, putting them on the same team. A correctly structured design charrette is one that allows sufficient time, spent in an atmosphere of mutual respect, for *stakeholders* to become *team members*. Researchers indicate that this kind of trust and commitment motivates team members to work together.[10]

On the other hand, a correctly structured design charrette *also* proceeds inexorably toward a mutually agreed upon and achievable deadline. The deadline is crucial. Given the complexity of the problem and the natural propensity of people to want proof before making decisions (proof that, as we saw above, can never come), an inducement to move forward is required. That inducement is the looming deadline. The unavoidable ambiguity and inconclusiveness of any sustainable design problem encourages an interminable design exercise. You have to end it at a fixed time to thwart this tendency. A fixed and commonly recognized deadline will help the group choose solutions—solutions that are selected in an atmosphere of consensus rather than "proof."

The Products of the Charrette Are Drawings, Not Plans
Design charrettes for sustainable communities produce *visions for space* rather than

Aerial perspective drawn during the Maple Ridge Smart Growth on the Ground design charrette. Drawings such as these give a better sense of the physical reality of a proposal than the "blob-on-a-map" plans usually provided to citizens. People are more able to project themselves into the space depicted and thus have a more realistic chance to appraise and comment intelligently on the proposal.

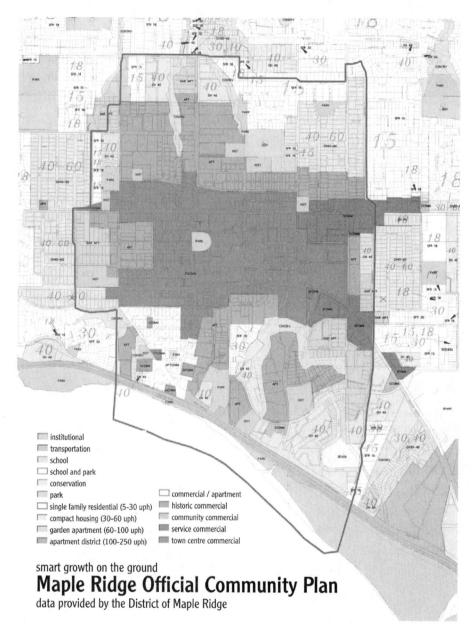

institutional
transportation
school
school and park
conservation
park   commercial / apartment
single family residential (5-30 uph)   historic commercial
compact housing (30-60 uph)   community commercial
garden apartment (60-100 uph)   service commercial
apartment district (100-250 uph)   town centre commercial

smart growth on the ground
Maple Ridge Official Community Plan
data provided by the District of Maple Ridge

A "blob-on-a-map" plan of the same area shown in the previous illustration. Plans like these are commonly used all over North America to determine the physical future of cities and districts. There is no way that citizens can project themselves into this plan and realistically appraise what kind of environment it would lead to. Absent that, the only reasonable reaction is indifference or fear.

plans for areas. Ground-level perspectives, aerial views, and highly detailed illustrative plans are the minimum requirements for sustainable community design charrettes. Although these kinds of drawings have severe limits, they are far more accessible to citizens than are the "blob-on-a-map" land use plans found at most planning hearings. Blob-on-a-map plans can depict land uses and traffic function only in the abstract. They say nothing about how the place might look, feel, or function. Blob-on-a-map plans edit out most of the sustainability variables and probably all of the subtle interactions between them. The design drawings produced at charrettes are not blob-on-a-map plans. Charrette drawings must depict more subtle sustainability issues, such as architectural ways of mixing income and family types on a street, or the amenity quality of protected stream corridors and their associated habitat zones. By creating drawings that depict sustainability issues in a form that is accessible to all, the charrette method ensures that the widest possible array of issues are manifested in the community vision.

2. Two Kinds of Charrettes

In the simplest terms, charrettes are of two kinds: visioning charrettes and implementation charrettes. Visioning charrettes produce illustrations of what it would look like if a district, city, or region were built sustainably. Implementation charrettes produce implementable plans for an area subject to regulatory change. There are blended versions of the two, of course, and we leave it to the reader to imagine these intermediate possibilities. We organize both kinds of charrettes. They require the same kinds of skills and staff support.

Visioning Charrettes

Visioning charrettes are speculative explorations of a possible future not directly tied to a government-regulated development or redevelopment proposal. Visioning charrettes may be of many types and focus at different scales, but they are most commonly conducted at the scale of the urban district. We ordinarily conduct visioning charrettes for sites between 200 and 3,000 acres in size, although we have successfully conducted a visioning charrette for a 1,500-square-kilometer (580-square-mile) urban region. A visioning charrette produces explicit depictions of what a community would look like if it were built in conformance with the sustainability principles spelled out in the design brief (the set of instructions given to the design team, described in chapter 3). The output of the visioning charrette is a series of compelling but speculative drawings for a real site, along with attendant text descriptions that help viewers to understand those drawings.

Who Should Be at the Table?

Visioning charrettes should have both design professionals and nonprofessional stakeholders at the table; however, when constituting visioning charrette teams, we believe that it is acceptable for design professionals (often supported by design students and aides) to constitute the majority of the participants and to play a leadership role. This is because visioning charrettes should produce beautiful and compelling drawings of a sustainable future—drawings that are complete enough to explain what a sustainable community might look like (and how it might work) without the need for elaborate written explanations. Based as they are in existing and emerging public policies aimed at promoting sustainable development, these images can provide officials and citizens with a clear image of what it would look like if their cities were actually built in conformance with those policies. Since actual built examples of socially, ecologically, or economically sustainable communities are exceedingly rare, a charrette that provides design professionals with the occasion to depict such communities can be of great value.

Images like this one from the Sustainable Urban Landscapes South Newton Visioning Charrette are an important means for demonstrating in tangible form how social and environmental policies come together on the site. This drawing shows how density targets can be met in a house form that will be appealing to residents while providing a mix of housing types for three families of diverse incomes. (Drawing by Ron Walkey.)

What Kinds of People Should They Be?

Design professionals at visioning charrettes must have certain qualities. First, they need to be able to draw. There are many brilliant community designers who cannot draw. They can be crucial members of the team, but they cannot replace designers with a "fast hand." Hand drawings are the crucial outputs of visioning charrettes, but they are more than mere products—they are a way of communicating with the other participants during the charrette itself (and with the larger public after the charrette is over).

Words alone are endlessly forgiving. It is far too easy to say in words how we might accomplish this or that sustainability goal; the test comes when you put pen to paper and draw the sketch. Suddenly there is just one option on the table, not the millions that words, however precise, would seem to allow. When a designer can put that option out, listen to critique, cross out lines and put in other ones, put a new piece of tracing paper over that and start over, massaging the form into something that gradually becomes a consensus proposal—that is the defining moment in any charrette. The person who can do that is a magician, conjuring up from the described impressions of the others an at first ephemeral, miragelike shadow of a shared world, eventually to be hardened into a buildable representation of what could be a real-world phenomenon.

Drawings are not the only way to represent landscape change. Various two-dimensional, three-dimensional, and computer-aided design programs are now available. We use them when appropriate, as well as noncomputerized techniques such as using chips to represent density or acres of public open space. But we also believe, for the reasons discussed above, that the hand drawing is irreplaceable. We have concluded that hand drawings will always be the core of the well-run charrette. No other medium so completely engages a group in its creation. Drawings create an inclusive atmosphere of collaboration akin to face-to-face conversation. Although other forms of conversation are now possible, such as e-mail, phone, or video conference, none of them will ever replicate the richness and complexity of face-to-face conversation. Drawings produced in the presence of others take the robust quality of face-to-face conversation and add to it the description of three-dimensional space. Other representational media—computer-based media in particular—lack this "conversation-like" quality.

But "conversing" with drawings is a rare skill. The ability to conjure images while still remaining capable of negotiating with teammates over this or that option already borders on the miraculous, but these talented people must also be patient and work

Talking while drawing is a unique and highly effective way to communicate. A skillful facilitator can draw and talk at the same time. Facilitators should insist that other people at the table draw too. It's not how pretty the drawing looks that matters, but how it facilitates insight, understanding, and empathy for the views of others. This behavior is not yet possible with computers.

well with others. Finding talented urban designers who can draw beautifully and who are also modest and patient is our most challenging project. Once we have found designers of this caliber, we use them again and again. They are irreplaceable.

How Long Should a Visioning Charrette Last? The Talk, Doodle, Draw Sequence
Our typical visioning charrette lasts a full week. There are variations on this length, but a week is the norm. One reason for this length is that the issues pertaining to sustainable community design are complex and require time to work out. Another reason is that it simply takes a while for the separate members of a team to become team*mates*. Not until the second day do they even begin to establish the necessary empathy, understanding, and respect for the value of their teammates. Only with empathy and respect in place can collective creativity be unleashed. We have a short-

hand way of describing this process and articulating the basic framework for charrette choreography: the "talk, doodle, draw" sequence. Since it takes days to establish empathy, we don't rush into drawings right away. We take what might seem a
large percentage of our time simply talking. We try to support this talk with whatever visual or map information is available, but the talk time is crucial. Talk time
builds trust and understanding within the team.

With interpersonal empathy established, we can move on to the "doodle" phase
of the charrette. In the doodle phase, ideas begin to gel in diagrammatic form, but
as doodles, they are intentionally ephemeral, and they can and should wind up "on
the floor" (i.e., as trash) before the charrette is over. During this phase, designers
work to conjure from the collective sensibility of the group a diagram that synthe-
sizes the various values held by team members. Such a diagram is more than the sum
of its influences. It is evidence of an emerging synthesis in form.

The final phase is the "draw" phase. The draw phase cannot really commence in
earnest until all members of the team are comfortable with the direction of the plan
and are happy to advance this or that individual portion or aspect of it on their own

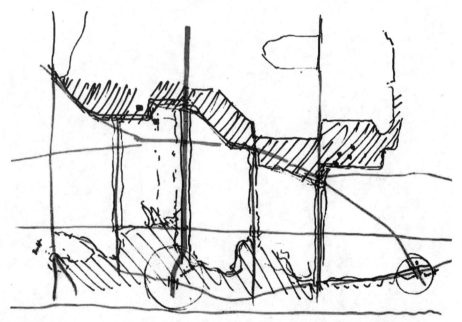

Through this very quick diagram from the doodle phase of Sustainable Urban Landscapes,
the Brentwood Design Charrette explores how water collection and management might serve
as a key driver of urban form. Drawings like this are what animate conversations at design
tables like the one shown in the previous illustration.

(or in small groups). During the rush to charrette completion, negotiations take place on the fly, with the deadline providing strong incentive to focus and act. The rate at which consensus can be achieved on a myriad of complex issues in such a setting approaches the miraculous. During this phase of a charrette, any negative attitudes about the fundamental beauty and goodness of the human spirit must crumble. The creative energy filling the room is both invigorating and draining at the same time. It is this extreme energy flow that leads to what Professor Douglas Kelbaugh, dean of the University of Michigan College of Architecture and Urban Planning, calls "post-charrette syndrome."[1] In his words, post-charrette syndrome is a consequence of the psychic demands of the charrette climax. It produces a trauma—a trauma grounded in euphoria, but one that extracts a psychic toll. In Professor Kelbaugh's humorous formulation, post-charrette syndrome is "the absolute certainty that you will never ever again agree to participate in a charrette, followed gradually by an increasing and eventually overwhelming urge to do it all again."

Participants in the Sustainability by Design Greater Vancouver Regional Charrette hold up the product of their draw phase, the work embodying the consensus forged during the previous talk and doodle phases.

What Is the Value of Visioning Charrettes?

1. THEY MAKE WORDS REAL

A visioning charrette allows participants to examine the probable physical consequences of meeting a particular set of sustainability objectives and targets. It makes ideas concrete, or at least much more concrete than if they were confined perpetually to mere words. Expressing your goal in pictures, in concrete three-dimensional proposals, is a way of resolving the inevitable contradictions between competing objectives. It is one thing to say that housing should be affordable, transit accessible, and environmental systems protected; it is quite another to locate enough housing to create a walkable, transit-friendly community without killing all the fish in the stream traversing the site.

2. THEY CREATE A COMMON LANGUAGE OF SOLUTIONS

Visioning charrettes can organize constituencies for more sustainable communities in a positive way. Often stakeholders are only given a chance to review proposals at public hearings, after their form is already set. At such meetings, environmentalists can only object to this or that encroachment on natural lands, neighborhood residents can only object to one or more aspects of a project that affects their area, and so forth. The typical public hearing format is good for only one thing: saying no, most often at great volume. Seldom are stakeholder groups given an opportunity to provide a picture of what they would say yes to if they got the chance.

Armed with diagrams and concept plans of site design, urban design, building design, and engineering design solutions to interrelated sustainability problems, the various players in the spectrum of constituencies that participate in the building of cities can begin to talk in a common language. That language is embodied in the pictures of the sustainable vision they have all contributed to. In short, visioning charrettes provide powerful communication tools—in effect, a new language—as well as directions for future policy change.

3. THEY ARE A NO-RISK PROCESS

Because visioning charrettes do not produce immediately implementable plans, they carry little risk. This fact has political advantages when one is working with risk-averse constituencies, and senior city staff members are notoriously risk-averse. Many upper- and middle-level city staff members know from hard experience that any departure from precedented norms will more likely lead to conflict and

These two drawings illustrate the resolution of an apparent contradiction between density and stream protection. The drawing above illustrates a high-density (25 units per acre) townhouse development across the street from a riparian zone. The street is constructed so as to allow water generated by the development to infiltrate and disperse before it gets to the stream. Drawing by Bill Wenk. The drawing below similarly explains how a road can traverse a stream with almost no effect if it is narrow enough and has a long enough span. (Drawing by Stacy Moriarty, for the Sustainable Urban Landscapes, Surrey Design Charrette.)

criticism than to consensus and praise. The author once served as director of community development and planning for the small city of Westfield, Massachusetts. I clearly remember looking at the telephone on my desk and hoping it wouldn't ring. In my experience, the phone rang only when someone out there beyond my office walls was angry and had enlisted a city councillor, or maybe the mayor, to bring their dissatisfaction to my attention. I remember thinking it ironic that I was so clearly being rewarded for doing nothing. When I did nothing, the phone stayed silent. It rang only when I actually did my job—angry phone calls came in only when I actually did some planning. This insight is crucial: the extremely stressful context within which senior city staff must survive is a huge impediment to change. Any model for advancing sustainability in North America must clearly recognize that cultural context and develop processes that do not exacerbate those stresses. Visioning charettes, since they carry none of the risk usually associated with changing officially regulatory documents such as official community plans or zoning ordinances, can provide stakeholder groups with a positive opportunity to work together with city staff, without the atmosphere of conflict that usually colors such debates.

4. THEY REVEAL POLICY CONTRADICTIONS

In our view, designs produced in visioning charrettes should always be framed against the existing public policy context for the region. The importance of this principle cannot be overstated. We are aware that others conduct charrettes for the express purpose of freeing themselves from existing policy or market constraints. They believe this allows them to produce more innovative solutions. Our experience suggests that whatever advantage might be gained by ignoring policy constraints is far offset by a loss of relevance for the plans thus produced. Market forces and public policies interact to produce urban landscapes. To ignore this fact is to flirt with irrelevance.

But how, then, does one make change if you are simply reusing the policy framework that already exists? In fact, we have found that the policy framework at the national, state, and regional level is most often highly supportive of sustainable development and thus provides a robust framework for any charrette design brief. But if that is the case, why does the North American city perform so abysmally against any realistic measure of sustainability? The answer lies in the contradictions between what policymakers say they want to do at the higher, more abstract, and distant levels of government and the development regulations imposed by lower-level officials.

The tools used at the lower levels of government are subdivision control ordinances, permit approval processes, and engineering standards. These crucial instruments are rarely examined under the sustainability lens. The charrette holds up such a lens, and it invariably reveals the profound contradictions between what we say we want to do, as expressed at the higher levels of government (provide affordable housing, save streams, enhance transit, and so forth), and what we are actually approving on a project-by-project basis. Only once these contradictions are unpacked can they be addressed. Absent this process, the various levels of government can operate for years without acknowledging that they are working at cross-purposes.

5. THEY ARE INEXPENSIVE

Finally, visioning charrettes can be a relatively inexpensive way to induce significant long-term change. *Relatively* is the operative word. Depending on their scope, our visioning charrettes have taken between 800 and 2,000 person-hours to complete. We won't accept projects for which less time is allowed. To do so would cheapen the process and too severely diminish the depth and quality of the outputs produced. To keep the math simple, a 1,000-person-hour charrette for which the billable rate is $100 per hour will cost over $100,000 to conduct. This is not an insignificant amount. Still, it is rare for municipalities to engage engineering consultants for less, even for relatively narrow studies such as those for traffic flow improvements at a few key intersections. Viewed through this lens, charrettes are remarkably efficient. A more conventional process to produce a comprehensive sustainable community plan, complete with adequate stakeholder participation, would cost much more. Finally, in our experience, most of the funding support for visioning charrettes comes not from the community that might most benefit, but from grants from private foundations and the higher levels of government. Foundations, provincial ministries, state agencies, and federal bureaus often support visioning charrettes, seeing in them an effective way to promote national and state objectives at the local implementation level. Higher levels of government and foundations may have a mandate to advance sustainable communities, as well as money to spend. The power to control the form of the community, however, is in the hands of local governments. Local governments do not ordinarily include global, national, or regional sustainability as part of their mandate and often feel too strapped for resources to take them on. Directing upper-level financial support to a visioning charrette can effectively shift local practices toward more sustainable results and thus meet the goals of higher-level governments and private foundations.

Implementation Charrettes

Implementation charrettes are conducted when there is a need for an implementable plan and associated regulatory documents. Anyone who has been a part of the processes governing land use change (usually in the form of some sort of rezoning) and the subsequent development of the redesignated lands (which requires complex engineering, environmental, transportation, and subdivision plans and regulatory instruments) knows how complex and time-consuming these processes can be. Various planning and engineering reports are invariably produced as a necessary precondition for investing the billions of dollars typically required to create new or retrofit old city districts. Implementation charrettes produce documents worthy of being incorporated into or replacing those reports. Thus they operate at a deeper level of responsibility and immediacy than visioning charrettes.

The major outputs of implementation charrettes are usually in the form of "local area plans" or equivalent. Jurisdictions all across North America have different names for and policies surrounding local area plans. Typically they focus on providing necessary roads, sewers, and water systems for newly developed areas. The more sophisticated also touch on community facility provision (such as schools and fire protection) and protection of environmentally sensitive areas. They typically inform a change to the zoning map and bylaws (most jurisdictions in North America except some in Texas use zoning maps to restrict land uses to specifically allowed uses). Most jurisdictions in North America are required to produce Official Community Plans. Official Community Plans outline in broad but mapable terms a community's intentions for land use, transportation, and utility servicing for new and existing areas. Local area plans should meet objectives set out in Official Community Plans. Local area plans produced at our charettes generally include land use planning requirements, urban design requirements, green infrastructure plans and regulations (i.e., open space, recreation, sensitive ecological area preservation, and low-impact engineering strategies), and engineering standards. Plans may incorporate or include by reference more detailed engineering, traffic, ecological protection, housing, or other types of technical plans.

Who Should Be at the Table?

Everyone who ordinarily has a role in the approval or implementation of a local area plan should be part of an implementation charrette. The participants will be developers, municipal planners, engineers, public safety officials, state and regional regulators, utility providers, and advocacy groups. As you can imagine, the list can be lengthy. We have developed the strategy of the "inner table" and the "outer table" to manage large groups of stakeholders, as discussed in chapter 5.

What Kinds of People Should They Be?

At implementation charrettes, there should be two kinds of people: stakeholders and design facilitators. Design facilitators should be chosen for the capabilities and human qualities described above for visioning charrettes. Good facilitation means being respectful of stakeholder positions, no matter how stridently and stubbornly they are expressed. Not everyone can do this. Even fewer good designers can.

Stakeholder slots should be held by the people ordinarily empowered to approve, develop, or provide input on site development plans. If you miss one of these crucial players, it is quite likely that there will be implementation difficulties eventually when the involvement of that person is required. This observation would suggest that organizers cannot choose participants for their collaborative skills, but must take whoever is in these slots of authority. There are exceptions, however: some units—a municipal planning department, for example—may have more than one potential participant to choose from. Selections can then be based on interpersonal skills.

Stakeholders should outnumber designers at an implementation charrette. Designers should act as design facilitators and not presume to have any authority over the site or its future. That authority lies, as it must, with the nondesigner stakeholders at the table. Thus design facilitators at implementation charrettes must, as in visioning charrettes, not only be able to draw like Michelangelo and have the humility of the Dali Lama, but *also* be skilled at translating everything from the technical requirements of sewer flows to the qualitative experience of place into a three-dimensional proposal, one that reflects the requirements and dreams of the participants who do have power—individuals who most often do not have a highly developed three-dimensional language of their own. Again, it can be seen how rare such facilitators are and how carefully they must be cultivated if discovered.

How Long Should an Implementation Charrette Last?

Implementation charrettes should be a minimum of four days long. Typically, if stakeholder participants know one another at all, they probably don't like one another very much. Municipal planners see developers as the enemy, as people who are always trying to get away with something and sneaking around to the city council behind their backs. Developers, on the other hand, see municipal planners as obstructionist, inefficient, and impossible to do business with in a timely way. Their complaints to the council, made out of frustration, are perceived unfavorably by city staff who are just doing their jobs. The only thing that the planning department and developers might agree on is that the city engineering department is worse! Thus many charrettes start off with a lot of protective body language and verbal trucu-lence. It will take more than a day to get beyond this atmosphere.

During the talk phase, the various perspectives of the participants must be care-fully and completely drawn out onto the table such that each stakeholder can "walk a mile in the moccasins" of the others. It takes at least a day and a half to get imple-mentation charrettes to the doodle phase. Spending additional time on talk often comes at the cost of less than fully developed ideas and drawings. For our implemen-tation charrettes, we don't worry too much about this. Because the group is largely nondesigners, and because there is a development pending for the site, it is better to spend time on negotiating an understanding between parties, using the drawings not as an end unto themselves, but as a way to achieve that goal.

Getting the right participants at an implementation charrette is always a chal-lenge. Charrettes are most successful when all of the key individuals empowered to make a development decision are at the table. Unfortunately, these are most often the very same people who can't imagine giving over an entire week of their time to any issue, no matter how important; the demands on their day are too pressing. Thus we frequently need to find a reasonable compromise between the value of high-level participation and the value of charrette duration of sufficient length to ensure suc-cess. We have experimented with many models, and we frequently choreograph charrettes in which stakeholders are present for two-thirds of the workday, with facilitators staying the whole day to "clean up the drawings" after stakeholders leave. Other variations are discussed in later chapters.

What Is the Value of Implementation Charrettes?

1. THEY GET US PAST THE "WINDOW OF NO"

Municipal governments in North America spend vast amounts of money putting people behind what we might call the "window of no." Development at the munic-ipal level is controlled by very specific requirements formulated as design, planning, and engineering standards. These standards must be specific enough so that they are not arbitrarily applied. Thus municipal regulators end up with little leeway when reviewing development proposals. A proposal either conforms to or violates an ordi-nance, bylaw, or engineering standard. Consequently, many municipal officials end up behind the "window of no," administering regulations aimed at preventing negative consequences to public health, safety, and welfare. It is nearly impossible to innovate in such an environment. A city engineer cannot unilaterally decide to change storm drainage standards to protect receiving streams; that falls outside his or her mandate. City engineers must ensure that what is built conforms to existing standards and "best practices" established in previous decades, no matter how much damage is done to receiving streams as a consequence.

What is the way out of this dilemma? Fortunately, there is a group at city hall that has all the discretionary authority necessary to change the way their city is built. Mayors and city councils have that power, but they seldom exercise it. Why not? Because they seldom feel equipped with the technical skills necessary to feel a high degree of confidence when departing from precedented norms, and they often do not fully understand their authority.

A properly choreographed implementation charrette can take advantage of this unused authority to spawn a more sustainable set of municipal standards and bylaws. In the first implementation charrette we held to produce the East Clayton Neighbourhood Concept Plan for the City of Surrey, British Columbia (see case study 1), our first and most important step was to ask the Surrey City Council to authorize our initiative. In their motion, they adopted seven principles for sustainable development to guide this work and further authorized city staff to explore the use of these principles as the basis for alternative development standards for the project. This authorization took the weight of responsibility for change off the shoulders of city staff, for whom it was an unrealistic burden, and placed it instead on the shoulders of the elected leaders of the community, where it belonged. By authorizing city staff to explore alternative standards, those leaders accepted whatever consequences might accrue from their explorations while providing "political cover" for the staff. Henceforth any controversy emerging consequent to the initiative would be shifted away from the staff. We strongly believe, for this and other reasons, that high-level authorization from elected bodies is a requirement for successful implementation charrettes.

The Surrey City Council also called for the staff in different departments to work collaboratively with one another. It may surprise some readers, but collaboration between municipal departments is rare. Yet creating integrated sustainable systems requires engineering standards, environmental protection regulations, and planning requirements to be tightly aligned. A duly authorized implementation charrette provides a city with the chance to align the policies of its various departments while protecting individual staff members from political repercussions.

2. THEY ARE POWERFULLY INTEGRATIVE

When most new districts are constructed, each issue area is handled on its own. Fire access is a case in point. Typically, fire officials are allowed to comment on development proposals only from the perspective of fire safety. These officials know from experience that their main authority is over the geometrics of road design (width, parking, curb radius at intersections, and so forth). Other planning issues are not their province. Consequently, fire officials have little say in broader issues of fire protection, such as road pattern configuration or fire station frequency. These latter two issues have a stronger influence on response times than road width, as studies have shown. Implementation charrettes create a setting in which these other, more influential factors can be put on the table for discussion, empowering fire officials to do a better job. At the same time, the roundtable context also brings some of the negative consequences of our hypothetical fire chief's usual regulatory responses into clear view. A very wide curb radius at an intersection may be a good thing for the hook and ladder truck if and when it needs to make that turn, but it's a bad thing for a kid who needs to cross at that corner every day. A hundred-foot diameter cul-de-sac bulb might be a good width to ensure fire access, but adding so much impervious surface would increase the impact on sensitive receiving streams. At an implementation charrette, the questions of keeping kids safe and fish alive are part of any decision. After a number of days at the roundtable, even the most ironbound fire chief will usually realize that there is much to be gained by looking for a holistic way to ensure fire safety while also recognizing how his or her decisions affect other sustainability issue areas.

In short, all of the sustainability objectives must be kept in mind all the time by all parties. This approach is entirely unlike the usual municipal process, wherein each reviewer comments on only one narrowly defined issue area. The result of this narrowly focused "silo thinking" is a dis-integrated world of completely separated solutions—a world within which each individual solution may be exquisitely rational, but the sum total of all those unconnected decisions is the self-evident illogic of sprawl. Implementation charrettes are designed to ensure that all issues are kept on the table at all times. Individual issues are advanced by the stakeholder participant who understands them best, and who in time understands how the issues dear to the hearts of other stakeholders might influence them.

3. THEY ARE FAST AND EFFICIENT

Our typical charrette lasts between four and seven days. There are variations (using just the mornings over two weeks, separating the charrette with a weekend,

This map shows response times and property damage from fires by municipality in eastern Massachusetts. The lower-density sprawl areas, which tend to have very wide residential streets, have generally slower response times and more property damage. Conversely, although they tend to have narrow streets, pre-World War II first-ring suburbs and urban areas perform better, largely because higher density allows construction of fire stations closer to all homes. Fire departments usually comment only on street dimensions and have little to say about community design, but better community design along the lines proposed in this book would also be likely to enhance fire access times.

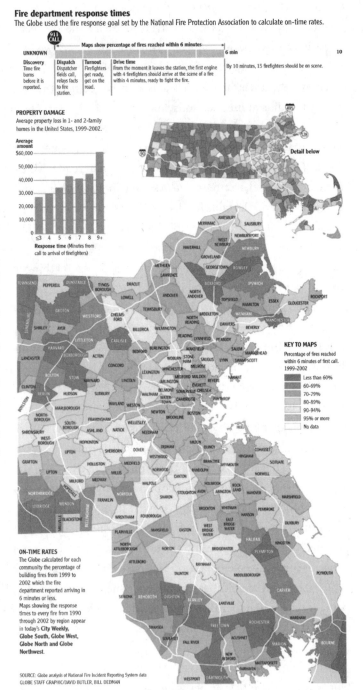

Fire department response times
The Globe used the fire response goal set by the National Fire Protection Association to calculate on-time rates.

PROPERTY DAMAGE
Average property loss in 1- and 2-family homes in the United States, 1999-2002.

KEY TO MAPS
Percentage of fires reached within 6 minutes of first call. 1999-2002

- Less than 60%
- 60-69%
- 70-79%
- 80-89%
- 90-94%
- 95% or more
- No data

ON-TIME RATES
The Globe calculated for each community the percentage of building fires from 1999 to 2002 which the fire department reported arriving in 6 minutes or less.
Maps showing the response times to every fire from 1990 through 2002 by region appear in today's **City Weekly, Globe South, Globe West, Globe North and Globe Northwest.**

SOURCE: Globe analysis of National Fire Incident Reporting System data
GLOBE STAFF GRAPHIC/DAVID BUTLER, BILL DEDMAN

having stakeholders leave earlier than facilitators, etc.), but this is the norm. Charrettes need to be several days long for all of the reasons discussed above. To those who are not familiar with the typical glacial pace of approval for even a modest subdivision, that may sound like a lot of time. But anyone who has been on either side of even the simplest approval process knows it is nothing. Approval processes, involving expensive engineering drawings, public hearings, various readings by the city council, and sequential review and amendment by a host of regulatory agents (at their "windows of no") can take years. Typically, the more complicated the project, the longer this process takes. Developers learn that the easiest way to lose money on a project is to do something out of the ordinary. Anything not previously approved runs the risk of engendering additional public concern and a longer period of regulatory review. In such an atmosphere, no innovation goes unpunished, as the innovator incurs increased project carrying costs associated with delay and an increased risk of outright project rejection.

Against this frustrating background, a week-long design charrette seems very efficient. In that time, all of the necessary regulatory approvals required are, at least in draft form, achieved. Additionally, the function of a public hearing is incorporated into the process, bringing citizens and neighbors in at the very first step. Although charrettes don't eliminate the requirement for a public hearing, they do ensure that community values are incorporated early on and that citizen proponents of the plan will be available to speak to council when the time comes. It may seem impossible to believe, but most of the plans produced in our charrettes have gone to public hearings, and eventually to council, essentially without opposition. This has been true even though most of our plans have proposed increasing final residential and job densities in the subject districts by more than a factor of five.

4. THEY ARE INEXPENSIVE

Depending on project scope, our implementation charrettes cost anywhere from U.S.$70,000 to $350,000. This is not an insignificant amount of money, but it is far less than is usually expended on traditional community planning processes— processes that are dis-integrated and lead to more costly sprawl. In later chapters we will detail more precisely where the money goes. Meanwhile, it should be acknowledged that municipalities are often disinclined to appropriate taxpayer money to pay for processes with which they are unfamiliar. City councils are more likely to approve a $200,000 engineering study of potential traffic impacts accruing from conventional development of a site than they are to initiate an untried process that promises to produce, but cannot ensure, results that more closely align with their sustainability goals. Nevertheless, we have successfully gained municipal financial support. More important, and more significant in dollar terms, has been the financial support emanating from foundations and higher levels of government. As mentioned above, higher-level governments and foundations often have a mandate to advance sustainable community development activities, but they seldom control the fundamental municipal actions that influence the outcomes of such activities. Charrettes can be an ideal bridge between the sustainable urban development missions of higher-level governments and foundations and the local-level officials who have the power to achieve those missions.

3. The Design Brief

The design brief, or design program, for a charrette is the set of instructions given to the design team. It provides specific numerical requirements and performance targets for the site. In many ways, the design brief or design program is more important than the final output of the charrette. The goal, objectives, principles, and targets in the brief can have a profound and positive influence not only on the outcome of the charrette, but also on the more enduring planning, urban design, and development policies of the host city and the region beyond, for the following reasons:

1. The design brief translates abstract sustainable development policy goals into concrete design requirements. For example, a very general goal of providing viable transit to all citizens gets translated into a requirement for minimum densities, an interconnected street system, and a bus stop within a 5-minute walk of all residences. Translating policy goals into specific design instructions will help policymakers understand the specific physical urban forms that might be the vehicles for achieving those policy goals. Policymakers are very rarely trained to make these links. The design brief makes them explicit.

2. The design brief provides a way for a broad range of stakeholders to participate in the charrette. Hundreds of people can help contribute to creating and approving the design brief during a series of workshops that precede the design charette as described in chapter 5, but only ten to twenty can effectively assemble around the design table at the charrette.

3. The design brief provides firm "rules of play" that participants in the charrette must respect. These rules ensure that the wishes of the larger stakeholder groups are respected at the charrette itself.

The design brief usually has four parts: the goal and objectives, the design principles, the numerical requirements, and the performance targets. Each of these four parts is described in turn below.

The Goal and Objectives

Charrettes have a goal. In any charrette, it is important to clearly state what the goal

RESIDENTS		
Total Site Area:	400 acres	160 hectares
Proposed Community Population	Minimum 9,000	Maximum 15,000
Proposed Total Dwelling Units	Minimum 3,200	Maximum 5,400
Residential Parking Standard	1.25 spaces per dwelling unit -.25 spaces per elderly or special needs un it.2 Parking can be on street or in surface lots.	
Gross Residential Density	Minimum 8 DU per acre, 20 DU per hectare	Maximum 14 DU per acre, 35 DU per hectare
OPEN SPACE	Minimum 60 acres (24 hectares) of unpaved public recreation and open space areas. Consideration of all environmentally sensitive lands for inclusion in open space system.	Maximum unlimited. Open space to include community and neighbourhood common spaces, playgrounds, parks, sports fields, conservation areas, community gardens, bicycle and walking networks,and other open, spaces.
PUBLIC TRANSIT	One or two light rail stops on King George Highway are anticipated. The exact locations of these stops have yet to be determined and should be suggested. Frequent bus connections from King George Highway to Surrey City Centre and the Sky Train station are presently available.	
COMMERCIAL		
Commercial Space	Minimum, 30,000 sq. ft. (2,800 sq. mtr.) per 1,000 population.	Maximum, 42,000 sq. ft. (3,900 sq. mtr.) per 1,000 population.
Commercial Parking Standard	750 sq. ft. or 70 sq. mtr. (3 spaces) per I 000 sq. ft. retail. On street and off street parking.	
LIGHT INDUSTRIAL/OFFICE		
Light Industrial/Corporate Office Space	25,000 sq. ft. (2,300 sq. mtr.) per 1,000 population.	
Service Office Space	16,000 sq. ft. (1,500 sq. mtr.) per 1,000 population.	
Light Industrial/Corporate Office/ Service Office Parking Standard	400 sq. ft. or 37 sq. mtr. (1.5 spaces) per 1,000 sq. ft. (or 90 sq. mtr.) office/light industrial.	

A sample section from the South Newton Design Charrette design brief. A design brief must be specific to lend credence to the charrette process and create opportunities to link the results to local policy. All numerical requirements are linked to existing policies and to the design principles underlying the charrette.

of the charrette is. In our charrettes, we take great care to get the goal right and to review it carefully with stakeholders. The goal almost always changes to some extent during this review. Here are two examples of goal statements that have survived this process, taken from two very different charrettes:

The Sustainable Urban Landscapes, Surrey Design Charrette
To demonstrate what neighbourboods and communities could be like if they were designed and built in conformance with emerging local, provincial and federal policies for sustainable development.

The Damascus Area Design Workshop goal:
The greater Damascus Area Community Design Workshop is an effort to create a regional model for the potential urban growth boundary expansion area that is environmentally sound, that provides a variety of housing and job choices for current and future residents, and fairly distributes the benefits and burdens of development among current and future residents of all incomes and backgrounds. This effort involves residents of the local area and region with a variety of interests and perspectives.

In the case of the goal statement for the Surrey Design Charrette, we needed to make it clear to ourselves and to others what the charrette would do and what it would not do. What it *would* do was depict what our neighborhoods would look like if we lived up to our public policy rhetoric. There was no intention of creating a buildable plan from this charrette. The goal makes this clear. The sustainable urban landscapes, Surrey Design Charrette was the visioning charrette that provided the basis for the later East Clayton Design Charrette, also in Surrey, BC.

In the case of the second goal statement, excerpted from the Damascus Area Design Workshop design brief, we needed to somehow capture the strategic objective of this unusual charrette, which occurred outside of any government mandate but was aligned with and parallel to a formal government initiative to plan and design this region. While the Surrey Design Charrette goal speaks largely to illustrative products produced, the Damascus charrette goal speaks largely to political processes engaged and influenced.

Rules for a Good Goal
- Ideally, a goal should be one sentence long—possibly a complex and long sentence, but just one sentence.

- Resist the temptation to have more than one goal. How can you run toward two goalposts at the same time?
- The goal should be such that each of the objectives that follow feel connected to it. For example, a goal that speaks only to transportation issues is not adequate if one of your objectives pertains to affordable housing.
- A good goal should somehow speak to both outcomes and process; that is, it should state that you will produce a certain outcome using a certain process.

The Objectives

Most simply, the objectives are the things you need to accomplish in order to reach your goal. They are often, but not always, measurable. A football analogy is often used. The goal is the touchdown; the objectives are first downs: you need up to nine of them for a touchdown. In charrettes it's the same: you need to meet a number of objectives in order to reach the goal. Often objectives are measurable in a way goals rarely can be.

In our work, we distill the objectives from already existing policies. As mentioned earlier, we believe that existing policies should always be used as the basis for the charrette. The most important way to incorporate these existing policies is through the process of identifying and articulating the charrette's objectives. Ideally, each objective will be directly connected to some publicly adjudicated or publicly reviewed policy. In our process, we collect all of the policy documents that could possibly pertain to the physical design of the subject site from federal, state, provincial, regional and local authorities. We then use this "policy base" as the source for all our objectives. Objectives without a basis in policy are most often excluded. For example, it might be instructive and inspirational to explore the use of windmills for power on a certain site. Sadly, it would be rare to find any support for implementing such a system in the policy documents informing the charrette. We are often tempted to include clearly sustainable design features in our charrette programs, such as wind turbines or extensive local agriculture. We usually opt for the more conservative route. If we can't find it in the policies, it's not in the design brief. We believe that maintaining a direct connection to already adjudicated public policies makes it much more likely that the charrette's design proposals will be implemented. If existing policies are closely adhered to, then the pictures produced at the charrette will depict what the world would look like if those policies were rigorously translated into urban design form. If everything depicted can be connected to a written policy, then what is drawn will not depict a utopian vision with little grounding in contemporary political circumstances. On the contrary, what is depicted is more rightly understood as *the necessary outcome of implementing current public policy*.

We specifically exclude subdivision regulations, zoning regulations, and engineering standards from the policy base, as these are typically the very things that are subject to review at the charrette. Often they can quickly be shown to contradict higher-level mandates for more sustainable communities in practice.

Here are two sample objectives each from the Surrey Design Charrette and from the Damascus Area Design Workshop:

Surrey Design Charrette objectives:
- To produce sustainable community design models for real British Columbia urban landscapes.
- To illustrate the design consequences of meeting disparate and often contradictory sustainability policy objectives.

Damascus Area Design Workshop objectives:
- To provide an independent, community-based design and planning process to inform UGB expansion deliberations and provide a positive model for growth for other parts of the region, the state, and the west.
- To ensure that there is a balance of jobs to housing in the area such that sufficient housing opportunities are available to households of all income levels that have a family member working in the area.

In the case of the Surrey Design Charrette, note how closely the objectives are tied to the goal by their mention of sustainable community design models and the illustration of the consequences of following existing policies.

Similarly, note the connection between the Damascus Area Design Workshop goal and the objectives listed. One objective speaks to the process of community involvement, clarifying and expanding on the last sentence in the goal. Similarly, the second one clarifies and expands on the goal's reference to job choice and distribution.

In addition to being based in policy, good objectives should have some formal implication for design. Many public policy objectives may be included in the documents reviewed, but not all of them will influence the final design. A requirement to eliminate smoking in restaurants may be a very good thing, but it will not materially influence the site plan for a proposed building. On the other hand, a policy requiring developers to provide adequate space for each resident to have a community garden will directly lead to an area requirement that the plan must eventually accommodate, requiring its inclusion in the design brief.

Rules for Good Objectives

- Each objective should be directly linked to other policy demands and referenced as such in the text.
- Each individual objective should focus on only one issue.
- Each objective should be one sentence long.
- The objectives should not be repetitive.
- No key issues should be left out.
- The objectives should describe general requirements, not specify numbers.
- The objectives should have formal implications for design.

Organizing Objectives by Category

Objectives have a tendency to proliferate. If a charrette has more than twenty objectives, that's probably too many. Twelve or thirteen is more manageable. However, complex urban landscape problems often require many objectives, and stakeholders often rightfully insist that a particular objective be included in the brief. When the list of objectives gets long, the need to organize objectives in manageable groups intensifies. The most obvious way to group objectives is into four categories:

1. Process objectives that speak to charrette process and political/educational strategy.
2. Ecological objectives that speak to protecting air, water, and habitat resources and reducing energy consumption.
3. Economic objectives that speak to the creation of jobs and reducing the costs for building and maintaining the urban infrastructure that supports them.
4. Social objectives that speak to the creation of equitable, attractive, affordable, and safe environments.

The basic sorting here is by the ecological, economic, and social dimensions of sustainability.

Dividing and Combining: From Objectives to Principles

In our charrettes, we are always struggling to maintain the integrity of the whole. The most compelling value of the charrette process is that it is inherently integrative and holistic.

Yet at the same time there are compelling reasons to explore individual issue areas. Most of the policy base comprises public policy initiatives aimed at addressing just one issue, be it fish protection or access to mass transit. The charrette must be designed to acknowledge this body of public policy work. As discussed above, the policies are first and foremost manifested in the charrette's objectives. But we find it useful, and perhaps crucial, to make one more attempt to reintegrate the individual issue areas prior to the charrette itself. We do this through the production and public review of design principles.

Design Principles

We have successfully conducted charrettes for which there were no design principles in the design brief, only a goal and objectives, as discussed above, and numerical requirements and performance targets, as discussed below. We have also used charrettes as the vehicle for generating design principles, producing them after examining the charrette's design proposal and extracting the implicit and explicit principles embodied in that design.

What Is a Design Principle?

A design principle for sustainable communities is a design response that intelligently integrates solutions for linked problems into one holistic rule—a rule that cuts across issue areas and, indeed, is not confined even to one of the three main dimensions of sustainability—ecological, economic, or social. Here are two examples of design principles from the Damascus Area Design Workshop:

Principle 1: Design complete communities

Complete communities are self-reliant, inclusive, and stable. Design a complete Damascus area with a fine-grained and diverse mix of housing, jobs, services, schools, parks, community facilities and natural areas—all within walking, biking, or very short driving distance from each other. Design a complete Damascus area so that people of diverse economic, social, and cultural backgrounds can live, work, shop, and play comfortably. Design a complete Damascus area in which involuntary displacement from family and friends is not the inevitable result of decreases in income.

Principle 4: Establish green infrastructure systems to bound, protect, and reinforce all neighborhoods

Green infrastructure integrates natural systems into the structure of a community—to reduce cost, protect stream flows, restore habitat, enhance commercial and residential development, and to make a place a home. Provide a green infrastructure vision for Damascus that protects those areas important to maintaining streams and habitat—including forested and steep slopes, ridgelines, riparian areas, floodplains, and large natural areas and wetlands—while bounding and enclosing new and existing communities.

A robust set of principles provides a point of orientation for participants and helps them evaluate options during the design charrette. Promulgating these principles as part of the design brief also gives a broad range of stakeholders an additional opportunity to adjudicate key pieces of the charrette process.

Principles are different from objectives. Objectives are hard, often measurable, targets that you either reach or you don't. Reviving our football analogy, an objective is reaching the 40-yard line in four downs. A principle is more like the strategy the team uses to reach its objectives: consistently relying on equal effort from all team members rather than a few stellar performances from star players, for example, might be a principle for success for a given team. Such a principle cuts across all the different parts of the game: offense, defense, passing game, running game, short yardage or long.

The principles used in our design charrettes are similar: they are holistic principles for success that cut across issue areas. If we unpack the two principles listed as examples above, we can see this. The principle calling for "complete communities" cuts across a host of issues, ranging from affordable housing to transportation. Similarly, the green infrastructure principle cuts across economic, social, and ecological dimensions of sustainability: green infrastructure is the more economical approach; the green systems should "bound and protect neighborhoods," so it is also social; and the principle demands the preservation of key green systems, so it is obviously ecological.

For a principle to pass muster, it must reinforce the goal and the objectives rather than contradict (or repeat) them. It must provide good guidance for what to do when the pen finally gets into our hands—when in doubt about where to put the mark, what does the principle say to do? How does it guide us? The complete communities principle tells us that the mix of land uses must be very tight, with a wide range of land uses within a 5-minute walk. It also says that those land uses should be linked by a network appropriate to pedestrians and not just cars, and that the community must include a variety of housing types for people of different incomes, ages, and family types.

Numerical Requirements

As the term suggests, numerical requirements have numbers tied to them. Numbers almost always direct typical municipal standards—the same standards that produce sprawl: density numbers that are usually too low, parking standards that are usually too high, and school size standards that are too big and too sprawling. Thus the numbers included in a sustainable community design brief are crucial. Some of the numerical requirements commonly included are described below. Different locations may have other numerical requirements, but these are the most basic ones.

Residential Density

The most important number in any sustainable community design brief will probably be the minimum residential density requirement. The higher the density, the lower the per capita use of energy for travel, infrastructure, and building conditioning costs. High density also saves farmlands from conversion to subdivisions, reduces the need for freeways in the region, and shifts the transportation mode mix toward transit.[1] For greenfield sites, we typically aim for a minimum gross density figure of ten dwelling units per acre (gross density is computed inclusive of streets and other public open space), taking this as the minimum threshold for sustainable communities. Communities built at this density or higher tend to have viable transit systems and schools, parks, and commercial services within walking distance.

When formulating the design brief, the positive results of density can and should be explored with stakeholders. When this provocative issue is unpacked, voices will be raised in opposition to higher density. They will argue that density has negative consequences, such as increased crime, traffic congestion, or greater impact on stream systems. These attitudes are deeply held and must be respected. It can be very useful at this stage to present models with densities at this minimum level and higher, but that still appeal to the "American dream" of single-family home ownership or village life. Homes on small lots, with and without secondary suites (rental units contained within single-family homes), can meet this minimum density threshold. Districts that have blocks of single-family homes near other blocks of townhouses or apartments can, on average, easily exceed ten dwelling units per acre. Even better is to mix these housing types on each block to make transitions to higher densities seamless and ensure a broader economic mix on the block. Density requirements can specify an average density on a block but also require some percentage of units to have a higher density, and others a lower density, than that average to ensure this outcome.

Density and Distribution of Other Land Uses

Density requirements for commercial and industrial land uses should also be listed in the numerical requirements section. We nearly always try to construct design briefs calling for a distribution of commercial space such that there can be at least a small corner store within a 5-minute walk of all homes. This requirement too

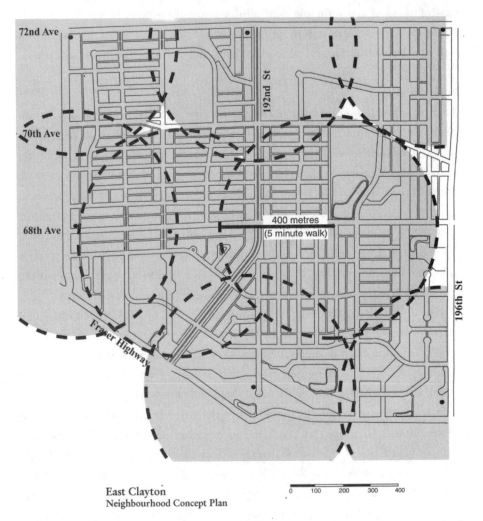

East Clayton
Neighbourhood Concept Plan

A 5-minute walking distance to commercial services and frequent transit is a fundamental rule for sustainable community design. North Americans will walk if they are provided with real destinations that matter to their daily lives. The most important walkable destination is not the park, but the neighborhood store. At densities in excess of ten dwelling units per acre, commercial services can be economically supplied within a 5-minute walk of every home. Lower densities probably will not provide sufficient customers within that radius to be viable.

stands convention on its head. The typical zoning map of most sprawling communities places neighborhood commercial convenience facilities (gas and go stores for the most part) within a 5-minute *drive*, not walk, of all homes.

The idea of changing the world of the 5-minute drive to the world of the 5-minute walk will provoke intense conversation in pre-charrette workshops. In many places this shift will be so dramatically counter to the prevailing sentiment that it will require substantial discussion to persuade the group to consider it. You may not succeed, but the issue must be addressed. Requiring sidewalks on both sides of all streets will do nothing if destinations for walking are not available. The most fundamental pedestrian destination in sustainable neighborhoods is the corner store.

The overall commercial square footage requirement will always be controversial. Most residential areas have little or no commercial space within or near them. Conversely, commercial space is most often oversupplied within some drivable distance. This distribution eventually creates landscapes that are entirely auto dependent because any purchase will involve a car trip to a sprawling and often congested commercial zone. Making more sustainable urban landscapes requires a redistribution of commercial space more broadly in the district. The question is how broadly. Our rule of thumb is that at least 25 percent of the total per capita commercial space allocation should be provided within the residential district. For the region of Vancouver, British Columbia, our recommendation is 10,000 square feet per 1,000 people within districts of 10,000 people or more. The largest single user of this neighborhood commercial space would be one or more supermarkets. The smallest commercial ventures would be the corner store or fruit and vegetable store. Hardware stores, restaurants, dry cleaners, video rental stores, and some niche commercial uses would occupy the medium-sized spaces.

The commercial square footage requirement also includes whatever neighborhood service office space the district can support (dentists, optometrists, accountants, etc.). In this category, a sustainable allocation of service office space would be about 5,000 square feet per 1,000 residents. Getting at least some of this space within a 10-minute walk of all residences would not be an impossible target, even though it is rarely found as an attribute of our present sprawling suburbs.[2]

Finally, there is the always difficult question of where jobs are located and how much space they require. Currently the standards that support sprawl operate to ensure that jobs are distant from homes, that they are inaccessible by pedestrians and mass transit, and that land devoted to jobs will yield very few jobs per acre. The proliferating "office park" landscapes where many, if not most, of North

America's new jobs are located exhibit a number of design flaws that thwart sustainable transportation and job equity goals. We try to address these problems through minimum floor surface/site area ratios for business uses and by establishing higher than currently assumed jobs per acre ratios for industrial lands, as well as by overlaying a maximum block size for industrial uses through the introduction of an interconnectivity standard of 600 feet (the maximum distance between through streets). In reality, most municipalities gear their industrial recruitment efforts almost entirely toward "hitting the grand slam home run"—the almost always unsuccessful attempt to lure an Intel or Saturn plant to town. Consequently, they zone very large industrial parcels (in excess of 40 acres) in the hope that an industrial golden goose will land. A quick review of aerial photos shows that new industrial and business buildings rarely require sites larger than 9 acres. Nine-acre sites fit inside streets that meet the 600-foot interconnectivity standard. We usually suggest that municipalities explore the benefits of such a standard and require a minimum FSR or FAR (floor surface ratio or floor area ratio; the proportion of floor area to site area) of at least 1.0. These requirements represent a dramatic, but we think not unreasonable or unachievable, departure from sprawl norms.

Determining the right numerical requirements, then, should be a major conversation at the workshops leading up to the charrette.[3] The right industrial development and transportation people need to be at the table to arrive at numerical requirements that help create communities where alternatives to the car exist while remaining realistically within current market constraints. Not an easy task.

Parking Requirements

Everything comes down to parking in the end. This apparently ludicrous assertion is unfortunately all too true. Many suburban municipalities demand that three parking spaces be located on a parcel (as opposed to on the street) for each new dwelling unit built. These same municipalities usually require roads wide enough for two 12-foot-wide lanes and two 8-foot parking bays on each side of the street. The results of these numerical requirements are the much-maligned sprawl streets where a full 40 feet of unoccupied pavement (unoccupied because the parking spaces on the street are never used, since there is so much on-site parking) invites the deeply cocooned SUV driver to drive at dangerous speeds.[4] Similarly, requirements for commercial parcels often call for between 2 and 3 square feet of parking stall space for every square foot of interior space, regardless of potentially available street parking space. These exaggerated requirements produce extremely low-density commercial

Very few industrial buildings actually require sites larger than an urban block, as these paired illustrations make clear. Above is a central Chicago industrial/business area where the buildings blend seamlessly into surrounding districts, fitted within the uniform block of the city grid. Below is a more suburban Chicago area industrial/business park. The individual buildings are similar in size to those in the central city, but much less densely arranged. The street network loads trips onto one main arterial road rather than distributing them into a street grid. Environmental regulations as presently implemented, as evidenced by the areas given over to retention ponds, decrease land use efficiency even further.

landscapes with FARs often as low as 0.3 net and 0.2 gross (when street space is included). Matters only get worse when municipalities layer in "landscape buffering" requirements in an attempt to mitigate these aesthetically brutal landscapes, further decreasing FAR and land use efficiency.

In our charrettes we suggest a reduction in parking standards to roughly half the present levels, look for ways to increase minimum FARs, and work with requirements for underground parking above a certain threshold density. Our parking assumptions begin with a belief that we can create landscapes that are at least 40 percent less auto dependent.[5] That conviction justifies reducing the parking requirements by a similar amount. Through this logic, we have promoted a parking standard for commercial uses of 750 square feet per 1,000 square feet of commercial space, with street spaces countable in this computation. If the blocks are small enough, and if parking spaces on rear lanes or back alleys where they exist are counted, the need for off-street parking in new commercial zones can be nearly eliminated. For residential uses, we recommend a standard of one on-site parking space per dwelling unit, with additional on-street spaces assumed to be available for additional family cars (if any) or the resident in a secondary suite. We always recommend parking on both sides of residential streets, but in the form of queuing streets where the travel lane provides a total width of 13 to 15 feet for two-way traffic (requiring approaching cars to slow dramatically to pass, but preserving full width for safety vehicles).

This system depends on an interconnected street grid forming small blocks. Finally, for residential densities over 18 dwelling units per net acre, we believe that underground or covered parking is economically viable in most areas and thus attempt to add it to the requirements in the brief.

Again, as in the previous cases, the numerical standards that regulate parking are controversial, and there will be strongly held opinions both for and against them. These opinions must be unpacked in the context of the larger assumptions of the charrette. It is difficult to meet sustainability objectives (which participants always want to do in the abstract, until, of course, they confront the need to change parking requirements) without attacking parking standards. Parking standards exert more influence over the specifics of land use and consequent transportation patterns than any other factor. An ever-increasing parking standard leads to an increasingly hostile pedestrian environment, which leads to ever-increasing auto dependence, which leads to an ever-increasing parking standard—ad infinitum. Working together to write and adopt the design brief allows stakeholder partici-

3.1 Queuing Streets

Queuing streets are narrow residential streets typical to older North American neighborhoods. They are usually between 24 and 28 feet wide measured curb face to curb face and allow parking on both sides of the street. This leaves a travel lane between parked cars that is too narrow for smooth, flowing two-way traffic. Cars approaching each other must slow and proceed with caution to pass, with one often migrating into an available parking space to allow the other to pass, thus the name queuing or "take your turn" streets. This kind of street is recommended by many sustainable community design experts as a natural way to slow traffic, reduce costs, improve aesthetic appearance, and reduce impervious surfaces.

pants the chance to unpack and then understand these nefarious linkages. In our experience, citizens from all walks of life are capable of understanding the subtle ways in which parking standards interact with sustainability and will support a substantial departure from the status quo—but not without sufficient time to discuss, debate, understand, and agree.

A typical commercial sprawl area north of Atlanta, Georgia. Commercial density in this landscape is very low. Less the 20 percent of the land area is covered by buildings and available for use (the gross FAR is 0.2). The other 80 percent of the land is consumed by the moving and parking cars.

School Requirements

Schools have been sprawling like everything else. In the Boise, Idaho, region, local school officials routinely call for 40-acre minimum sites for new schools. Schools on such sites cannot be reached from homes on foot in less than 10 minutes; it takes that long to walk from one corner of the sun-scorched playground to the front door. Large minimum acreage requirements, usually accompanied by large minimum school size requirements, condemn kids to be driven or bused to school and to spend the day in a school with too many kids to be known as individuals. The Small Schools Initiative of the Bill & Melinda Gates Foundation is one significant attempt to counter this destructive trend.[6] If the local policies are at all flexible, we commonly suggest a maximum 400-student standard on sites smaller than 10 acres (or two typical blocks) or less.[7] Elementary schools of this size, located amid a density of a minimum 10 dwelling units per acre, can be practically provided within an 8-minute walk of all homes (the residential population within that 8-minute-walk catchment area will be 5,000 residents or so).

As in the case of parking standards, suggesting substantial downsizing of the standards for school site size may prove controversial. The school district may have spent thousands of hours and millions of dollars committing to a strategy of bigger schools, spurred by what they consider to be a very compelling set of motivations, but we doubt that community cohesion, walkability, and regional sustainability were high on their list. They must be placed on that list. Schools are such a linchpin for communities and community functions that the topic must be engaged and progress must be made. Charrette planners must facilitate conversations that reveal the connections between the sizes of schools and their sites and other related sustainability factors—notably child safety, creation of healthy opportunities for daily walking, cutting the costs of school buses, and reduction of traffic congestion during morning commute times. Broader and more substantive conversations about the damaging effects of sending kids to schools that are too big and too anonymous may be even more compelling to some participants, but run the risk of engendering even more resistance from officials who have adopted an opposing view.

It is crucial to establish the right numerical standards for at least the categories listed above—the reader now probably understands why. The devil is in the details; with sprawl, the devil is in the numerical standards. Densities, jobs per acre assumptions, commercial distribution targets, and FAR requirements are all numbers. Get them wrong, and you get unsustainable auto-dependent neighborhoods that pollute water and air and fail to provide affordable housing for even half of those who need homes. Get them right, or at least a lot better, and we have a fighting chance at changing the status quo before it's too late.

Performance Targets

Public policy is often stated in nonnumerical terms. Policy objectives such as "provide affordable housing," or "ensure that stream habitat is protected" are of a different order and type than numerical requirements; thus we place these performance targets in a separate section of the design brief and handle them differently. Our first task in establishing performance targets is to pore through what we call the "policy pile," pulling out public policy performance targets from disparate and usually unrelated documents. Policy piles for any developable region can be quite tall; they usually measure in many feet for our projects. Someone must take on the arduous and time-consuming task of poring through each document looking for the key data and conclusions. The task is made somewhat easier if the documents include clear goals, objectives, and policy targets. We sort the key elements into categories, usually roughly correlating with the ecological, economic, and social dimensions of sustainability. However, each charrette provokes some variations on this theme. For the Surrey Design Charrette, for example, the performance targets were sorted into The Land and Water, Built Form, and Energy.

Once sorted into these categories, similar targets from different sources are collapsed into a single performance target. In this way we produce as short a list as possible, a list that both honors the depth of previous policy work and is manageable by the charrette team. As you might suspect, there is as much art as science to this task. As an example of what such performance targets might look like, here are the performance targets from the Surrey Design Charrette in the Built Form category:

1. Housing Equity

Provide a balance of housing types that meet the needs of a range of ages and lifestyles and are affordable to groups and individuals within a wide range of incomes. At least 20 percent (minimum of 720 units if 10,000 persons inhabit the site) of the housing shall be for persons with family incomes in the bottom third. Income statistics for Surrey residents are listed in the appendix, as are examples of market and subsidized housing types which are normally provided for this sector.

2. Special Needs Housing

Provide adequate special needs housing (seniors, disabled, family crisis victims, etc.; Surrey demographic information is in appendix).

3. Safety
Employ proven methods of enhancing community safety and sociability.

4. Integration of Land Uses
Create a mix of building and land uses, integrating residences, work, shopping, and services (community, professional, commercial, and institutional).

5. Access to Transit
Ensure that most persons live and work close to transit and services to reduce dependence on the automobile, promote pedestrian activity and bicycle use. Note the footnote numbers for each target, which link each target to a footnote identifying the documents and pages in the policy pile where support for the performance target can be found. In many cases, a single footnote will link to many documents.

Again, this practice is a demonstration of our strongly held belief that the charrette is a much more powerful instrument for social and physical change if the organizers can amply demonstrate the connection between the final design results and the public policies promulgated by citizens and their elected leaders. For further examples, readers may refer to the appendix, where links to full design briefs are provided.

Required Products List
Every design brief package should include an easy-to-use pullout list of required drawings, calculations, and explicatory text. We have learned that it is important to clearly list the required products and to make sure that those products are generated. To ask for too many products is the worst thing you can do; do this and you can't be sure what you will get at the end of the charrette. Only slightly worse is to be unclear about the required products, trusting the team to make up their own minds about what to provide. In this second case, you also won't know what you will get at the end. The short list of required products should always include the illustrative plan, detail plans, and infrastructure diagrams. Additional items in order of importance might be perspective sketches, street and site cross sections, building typology explorations, and block and parcel explorations.

Drawings will be the main output of a design charrette, but always insist on a written report; don't insist, and it won't get done. Make sure that the team elects an official recorder to document outcomes in words—words that explain and expand on the drawings. There is always someone on the team who can't draw and is therefore at loose ends on the last day of the charrette. We provide an electronic template for the report in the form of a questionnaire. We write questions in text boxes with spaces below where participants can provide an answer. This template allows for commonality in the case of multiple-team charrettes and allows the work to be easily divided up among team members in the case of single-team charrettes. The questions are typically organized in parallel with the design objectives; for example, the objective "Ensure that there is a balance of jobs to housing in the area such that sufficient housing opportunities are available to households of all income levels that have a family member working in the area" becomes the question "How did your team establish a balance between living wage jobs and affordable housing in the area?" The template can also ask simple questions that pertain largely to the numerical requirements, such as, "Were you able to accommodate all of the housing required at the given densities?" If you fail to ask this fundamental question, you might never know for sure.

Points of Departure for Design

Sometimes a charrette challenge simply seems too big, even after every effort has been made to simplify it. In the case of the Damascus Area Design Workshop, a charrette for a 25,000-acre proposed Portland (Oregon) area urban growth boundary expansion, we imposed an additional level of structure: we created three subteams and gave them each a different "point of departure for design." We asked each subteam to produce a complete design for the site using the common design program. What distinguished each subteam was their given "point of departure for design." Members of the "Home" team were asked to use those objectives and targets most associated with the creation of complete communities as their point of departure. Similarly, the "Go" and "Green" teams were asked to use the objectives and targets associated with getting around and with environmental protection as their respective points of departure. The Damascus Area Design Workshop Instructions to Design Teams, excerpted below, provides examples:

1. "GO" TEAM

OH MAN, WHAT A HOT POTATO!

Of all the issues that confound the question of expanding urbanization into the Damascus area, transportation is probably the most problematic. The Sunrise Corridor Proposal has provoked passion and anxiety for over twenty years now and is still not resolved. This is only one of the contentious questions surrounding transportation. The Damascus Concept Planning Study (Damascus Study) anticipates a need for over 10 miles of new five-lane suburban arterial roads to serve the 30,000 new residents of the study area. This falls far short of the minimum 100,000 residents this workshop is allowing for! Would 30 miles of five-lane road be required for this number of residents? Certainly, this workshop will not put an end to the many questions associated with road design and construction. What the workshop can do is provide an opinion about how to best coalesce objectives for moving in and through the region into a livable, affordable, and ecologically sensitive urban design framework. To cite just one example, the Metro Council has recently adopted a 530-foot maximum road interconnectivity standard. However, the Damascus Concept Planning Study (Damascus Study) assumes that such a standard cannot be achieved in this zone due to fractured ownership and topographical barriers. Does the team agree with this position?

An alternative vision would make dramatic changes to the trip numbers used to generate conclusions about the number, lanes, and length of major suburban arterial roadways.

The Damascus Study also assumes that all east/west traffic must be carried on a much-enhanced Sunrise corridor running parallel with 212. Does the team agree that there are no other possible options for east/west travel? This team can and must offer an opinion in the form of a street network diagram similar to the one shown on page 56 of the Damascus Study. This is a significant charge for this team.

Thus each team attacked the problem from its own point of departure, but also had to satisfy all the other demands of the program in a holistic way. The challenge is to allow teams to focus on complex and fundamental issues while not losing sight of the whole. Lose this holistic view, and the charrette falls back into the trap of silo thinking. The full Damascus Area Design Workshop design brief is accessible via a Web link in the appendix.

Cheat Sheet
There is an inevitable tendency toward "brief bloat." In a public process, in which so many issues arise and the needs of so many stakeholders must be incorporated, it is natural for the design brief to grow and grow. Our shortest design brief ever was about 2,000 words, not counting footnotes. That was one of our first, done with lim-

ited stakeholder involvement. One of our longest, for the Damascus Area Design Workshop, was over 10,000 words, with another 5,000 words or more in the explanatory footnotes; that one was the product of a very long process of stakeholder engagement.

Unfortunately, as design briefs get less brief, they also get less useful. Participants can no longer simply pick them up and flip to a directive as they work; the document itself is too unwieldy. We try hard to keep our design briefs short, but failing that, we provide participants with a "cheat sheet." A cheat sheet, as the name implies, is an attempt to boil down the whole design brief into one or two pages. It is usually organized in the form of a matrix, with the objectives on the left and columns that might identify numerical requirements and performance targets for each objective. An example of the "cheat sheet" used at our Southeast False Creek charrette is accessible via a Web link in the appendix.

Strategic Targeted Research

Strategic targeted research as discussed in chapter 5 in the section on technical bulletins can and should be made part of the design brief. This crucial research must be on the table and in the face of participants. An overwhelming amount of information informs a typical charrette—simply providing the policy pile and any relevant reports for participants is no guarantee that they will be read. It is best to take the key pieces of research that already synthesise key features of that library in digestible form, and isolate those and only those research items in the design brief.

Appendices

An appendix to the design brief might contain certain information not produced by the charrette organizers; key demographic background information that justifies housing targets would be one example. Sample drawings, which may be useful for giving participants an idea of what they are expected to produce and a model for how to produce it, can also be provided in the appendix. Always remember that the capacity of participants to digest reams of information is limited. The talking and the drawing that captures the results of the talking are the key products of the charrette. Don't do anything to compromise that outcome, including expecting participants to read too much.

4. The Nine Rules for a Good Charrette

The nine rules below form the substantive core of this book. If you remember nothing else, remember these rules. They are easy to understand and easy to remember, yet they represent the collective wisdom and experience of hundreds of individuals who have worked with us over the decades, all struggling hard to come up with a new paradigm for making community planning and design decisions. The nine rules are listed below, followed by a more lengthy discussion of the rationale behind each of them.

Rules for Successful Sustainable Community Design Charrettes
1. Design with everyone
2. Start with a blank sheet
3. Build from the policy base
4. Provide just enough information
5. Talk, doodle, draw
6. Charrettes are jazz, not classical
7. Lead without leading
8. Move in, move out, move across
9. The drawing is a contract

The reader should memorize these rules. Reading the rationale below each rule should help in that effort.

Rule 1. Design with Everyone

Our first and most important rule is "Design with everyone." The usual public review process is an ineffective way of engaging citizens in decisions. Municipal officials will always defend their public process, yet these same officials will be dismayed when it leads to confrontation with what they perceive to be uninformed NIMBYs (which stands for "not in my backyard"; i.e., people exhibiting knee-jerk opposition to change). Public hearings are usually held in a formal hearing room, where consultants dressed in expensive suits stand at the front of the room and present elaborately illustrated plans to skeptical citizens assembled in rows below. The hour or two devoted to the public hearing is too short for substantive critique, and it is *far* too short for productive collaborative problem solving; proposing and testing alternatives or evaluating and negotiating community benefits is impossible in such a context. All citizens can do is voice their objections, which they often do stridently. Elected officials at the local level are notoriously cowed by the appearance of twenty or more angry voters, even though that number might constitute a tiny fraction of the constituents actually affected by their actions. Thus they most frequently vote to appease their constituents, making it increasingly difficult for developers to heed the needs of the larger community or to capitalize on untapped demand for more intensive land uses. In certain metropolitan areas, notably the Bay Area of California, the inability of local jurisdictions to withstand citizen objection to intensification of land uses has frozen what would otherwise be robust markets for densification and infill.

What can be done about this seemingly intractable problem? We suggest that the problem is neither knee-jerk opposition to change (NIMBYs) nor the shortsightedness of public officials in the face of opposition. The problem is that current processes separate the world into two camps: people who have a role in designating the changes that will occur in a given landscape and those who don't. We also suggest that even within the group that has design authority, the design tasks are so thoroughly dis-integrated (with engineering separate from planning, planning separate from architecture, architecture separate from riparian protection, and so forth) that a balkanized result is almost certain. The ultimately balkanized proposal cannot be expected to inspire support when the process that led to its creation so artfully frustrates any possibility of design integrity. The solution? The solution is to design with everyone.

How is it that everyone can design? Professional designers spend years learning their craft. How is it possible for nonprofessionals to participate as equals in a design process? The answer is simple: Design is more a way of thinking than a specific set of technical skills. Design is a state of mind in which ambiguity is accepted. Most problem-solving modes proceed linearly and depend on the orderly execution of certain technical tasks or rational steps. That is fine if variables are limited. But design problems always have a host of variables and therefore an infinite variety of possible solutions. The design process is therefore necessarily and inherently qualitative, depending on intuition and judgment to select from alternatives. Intuition and judgment, by their nature and by definition, are inherent human qualities as opposed to acquired skills. Certainly training can hone these qualities, and certain people are endowed with more than their share of both. But most individuals have enough intuition and judgment to add value to a well-designed charrette effort.

Rule 2. Start with a Blank Sheet

Imagine this moment: A 4 x 6 foot base map of a large site sits ready on the table. The base map is a 1:1,000 scale orthographic aerial photo of the 500-acre site. Participants are gathered around the big map, chatting, possibly having just come from a site tour. Finally, someone takes a 4-foot-wide roll of tracing paper and carefully rolls it over the map. I have witnessed this many times. Conversation slows, or even stops. Everyone realizes, perhaps for the first time, that the paper is blank—both literally and figuratively blank. The blank sheet expresses both possibility and challenge. Staring at it begins the process of galvanizing the team. No one individual at that moment feels adequate to the task. Even we, the organizers—who have done this many times—feel inadequate at this moment. But the organizers have one advantage over the rest: we have seen this process work every time. Somehow the blank sheet gets filled, through some strange human alchemy, with a shared vision.

The blank sheet is important both as an actual challenge and as a symbol of the absolute authority of the team. The team must feel empowered and challenged at the same time. If the sheet has too many, or even any, decisions already depicted, then the rationale for the charrette is weakened. If basic land uses have already been assigned, then opportunities to explore mixed-use strategies, typically the hallmark of sustainable communities, are limited. Things are worse still when basic road infrastructure decisions have been imposed—typically as a consequence of a previous study based on transportation models and strategies that necessarily lead to the auto-dependent sprawl the charrette intends to avoid. If land use and transportation decisions have already been made, the charrette has lost its meaning. Participants will quickly understand this. Any commitment to a challenging collaborative task, a necessary condition for success, will be severely compromised.

Day one: Confronting the blank sheet. Someone will eventually make a mark.

Admittedly, the previous paragraph is idealistic. Often previous decisions made for the site will not be reversible or subject to review. Certain elements of the context, or construction projects planned or under way, will produce unpleasant and negative pressures on the process. But *starting with a blank sheet* is nevertheless an important ideal to strive for. Organizers should argue forcefully with project sponsors to get the sheet as blank as possible, and they should refuse to facilitate charrettes where, in their judgment, too many options have been foreclosed.

Rule 3. Build from the Policy Base

As discussed in chapter 3, charrettes must be firmly grounded in existing policy. Ignoring existing policy renders charrettes academic at best and counterproductive at worst. Policy at the national, state, provincial, regional, and local level is generally compatible with sustainability goals. A direct link can and should be made between policy emanating from these levels of government and each element of the design brief. At first glance, this rule may seem to contradict rule 2 above. In fact, the two rules are a necessary complement. The blank sheet would be entirely too daunting a challenge without an explicit set of program requirements, while the program requirements would be pure fantasy if not tied by many threads to existing policy.

Program requirements are not real until they are tied to the site. It is easy for the design program to state that housing must be dense and affordable on the one hand and that stream function must be protected on the other. It is not until you try to design for both results simultaneously that the inevitable conflicts between these two laudable objectives emerge. And only *design*, as defined in chapter 1, can elevate and resolve these conflicts through an iterative and collaborative process of give and take, of synthesis and synergy, of empathy and understanding. Thus rules 2 and 3 are linked in a dialectical way; they are two sides of the same phenomenon, like night and day, hot and cold, rational and intuitive.

Rule 4. Provide Just Enough Information

In our description of rule 1, we suggest that the design process is propelled by intuition and judgment. But if intuition and judgment are the engine of the charrette, information is the fuel. Any site development project will be influenced by many technical and policy issues, many of which will themselves have been the subject of elaborate and expensive previous studies. These studies may range from riparian habitat inventories to marketing studies for housing to job growth projections to demographic analyses to social needs assessments.

This information should be channeled to three destinations. First, if the information is concise, it should be made part of the design brief. An example might be the allowable rate of stormwater discharge from a site as determined by the authors of a watershed protection study. Second, if the information is considered vital but cannot be adequately compressed to fit in the design brief, a technical bulletin can be supplied. This easily digestible document of four to six pages is designed to inform rather than slow dialogue (see the appendix for Web links to technical bulletins on a variety of topics). Third, all of the information in the "policy pile" is assembled into a charrette "library" of relevant technical studies and policy documents.

The key is to provide just enough information and no more. Too much information produces decision paralysis. Too little information produces bad proposals. Determining how much or how little information to provide, and in what format, is more art than science. From our own experience, we know that participants will digest very little background information prior to the first day of the charrette, no matter how far in advance it is provided. Consequently, vital information must be separated out and made concise enough to be digested during the charrette. To provide the participants with a deeper understanding, and to ensure that they will base their decisions on a robust knowledge base, we depend on the individual stakeholders, one or more of whom will probably have expertise in the technical or policy area in question.

Rule 4, then, is cautionary rather than prescriptive. It merely points out the dangers of providing too much information, and too little. There is no neat solution to this conflict. Ultimately you must have faith in the collective intelligence and experience of the charrette team. Your responsibility as organizer is to reinforce their knowledge with whatever reference information might deepen their understanding but not slow their progress.

Rule 5. Talk, Doodle, Draw

Talk

Participants should initially talk about their ideas, progressively move to doodling, and finally draw out their vision. There is a danger in rushing this process. It takes a certain number of hours, or even days, to unpack the issues embodied in even a simple charrette program. It takes time for the various stakeholders to offer their opinions about the problem, and just as important, for the stakeholders to get to know one another better. We often say that it "takes two days for stakeholders to become team members," and it does. The process of transformation from stakeholder to team member that occurs during the talk phase can seem maddeningly unproductive to the action-oriented designer, particularly in light of the ticking clock and the looming deadline. But rushing into fixed design decisions before this process has unfolded is an all too common mistake.

Stakeholders must also become *designers*. The transformation from stakeholder to designer also occurs during the talk phase. A designer is *one who designates*, as we pointed out in our discussion of rule 1 above, using a problem-solving process driven by intuition and judgment. But the average participant does not come to the charrette knowing this. Participants are more likely to think that acting as a designer requires far more technical competence than they possess. As the week-long charrette unfolds, participants gradually become more comfortable thinking of themselves as designers. From the other side, design facilitators at charrettes must create an initial culture of collaboration in which everyone is accepted as a designer, rather than "solving the problem" on their own. Again, skillful, empathetic, and respectful facilitation is crucial. Design facilitators that embody all three qualities are exceedingly rare and when discovered should be cultivated.

Most of the talk during the talk phase is at the *table of the whole*—the "big table" where the whole team gathers. Issue-focused subgroups may occasionally be formed (on transportation, community design, or green infrastructure, for example), but these subgroups should convene for a short time and then reconvene at the big table, reporting back their conclusions in a way that enhances the broader dialogue rather than leading to silo thinking.

Doodle

Eventually talk must turn into drawings. The intermediary step between talk and drawing is the doodle or diagram. Doodles and diagrams were discussed in chapter 2, but in the context of this rule, it is important to emphasize that they are tools for turning talk, which can be endless, into concrete decisions. Diagrams are loose enough to allow for various interpretations while still imposing a discernible order on all or a part of the site. In addition, doodles and diagrams are not intimidating—anyone can doodle. Stakeholders can start to give form to the site with their own hands if the atmosphere of doodling is welcoming and facilitators understand how crucial it is for stakeholders to contribute directly as authors of the design.

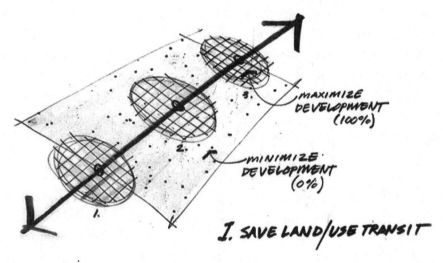

Product of the doodle phase of the Brentwood Design Charrette in Burnaby, British Columbia. During the doodle phase, concepts can be quickly explicated in visual form and in relation to the subject landscape. Diagrams allow ideas to be tied to the land without getting lost in exact site constraints. (Diagram by Kim Perry.)

Draw

The draw phase commences only after the stakeholders are sure that the drawings will reflect a previously arrived at consensus. I have managed charrettes at which teams came excruciatingly close to the end of the charrette without consensus on basic issues (ironically, this seems most likely to occur when there are more technical experts on the team than usual). Eventually they arrived at consensus, leaving little time for elegantly rendered drawings. But the drawings are the evidence of consensus, rather than an end in themselves. Thus, even though the draw phase was rushed, the charrette was successful.

During the draw phase, the table of the whole can and should be broken down into separate task-oriented tables. In this case, the facilitator's role becomes that of coordinator, making sure that the designs and products emerging from each subtable are compatible with all the others. We make sure that there are three or four "fast hands" at every charrette, individuals who are not only good designers but also draw effectively and expressively. But as long as we have a few very clear and professional-quality drawings to explain the overall design idea in a compelling way, we are happy to have other drawings that are less well rendered and in some cases very crude. These other drawings can be as rich in content as more professional ones while also allowing less skilled draftspeople an important task to complete during the draw phase.

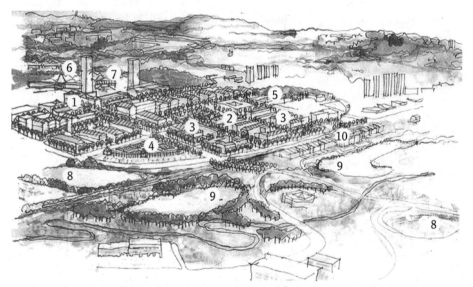

Product of the draw phase of the Brentwood Design Charrette. Here the drawing is still quick but very specific in locating design elements on the land. This drawing can be produced only after consensus is reached, usually during the last day of the charrette. (Drawing by Kim Perry.)

Rule 6. Charrettes Are Jazz, Not Classical

Rule 6 suggests that design charrettes are like playing jazz. Jazz musicians often start with an organizing theme to begin and return to, with unstructured and extemporaneous solos sandwiched between. Jazz is therefore much like design: it works with ambiguity and is not searching for perfection, but rather for something fresh and unpredictable. Like jazz, design charrettes are propelled by inherent skill, intuition, and judgment. Jazz can reach unpredictable creative destinations that are impossible in classical music. This does not mean that design charrettes and jazz are random. They are rather a creative chaos, like fractals in nature—a process that seems random at first but eventually organizes itself into a beautiful pattern. The fractal patterns that emerge in nature, in jazz, and in charrettes result from the interplay between a set of fixed rules, dialectically related to opportunities for variation and creativity.

The analogy with jazz has proved particularly useful in our work. Stakeholders become more relaxed about this intentionally open process once this analogy is presented, and facilitators are less anxious knowing that the rules contained in the design brief and the physicality of the site will ultimately provide order.

Rule 7. Lead without Leading

Rule 7 goes hand in hand with rule 6. It pertains to how charrette facilitators should conduct themselves before and during charrettes. To lead without leading is one of eighty-one major lessons captured in the *Tao Te Ching*, written by Lao-tzu twenty-six centuries ago. This short text is a primer on the proper conduct of life, government, and warfare. Here is the full text of its chapter 17:[1]

> The best leaders are those the people hardly know exist.
> The next best is a leader who is loved and praised.
> Next comes the one who is feared.
> The worst one is the leader that is despised.
>
> If you don't trust the people,
> they will become untrustworthy.
>
> The best leaders value their words, and use them sparingly.
> When she has accomplished her task,
> the people say, "Amazing:
> we did it, all by ourselves!"

Leading without leading in charrettes is thus about silences. When all members of the design team are fully engaged and actively collaborating, the leader, or facilitator, leads by remaining silent. She lets the process take its course. But the leader remains watchful for signs of disturbance: watchful for stakeholders left out of conversations and thus inclined to become increasingly alienated from the process; watchful for an overly aggressive and dominating presence in the group, a presence that makes dialogue impossible; watchful for a process that veers away from the objectives set earlier by the group.

Leading without leading also means asking the right questions: asking how a certain action supports the objectives of the group; asking how a certain response to transportation concerns might influence affordability, or aquatic systems; asking how the group thinks it is doing and how confident it is that it can reach consensus on all of the key issues. All of this listening and questioning is a quiet activity, characterized by much more listening than talking, and by talking in a calm manner.

But there is one more action that the leader who leads without leading must take. There are inevitable times when the group slows to a halt, dragged down by the complexity of the challenge or even by simple fatigue. Into these voids the leader must drop words. At dinner parties, the most able host knows that her skills are most needed at times when the table quiets. Extreme grace is required to take these moments of silence and break them, knowing that any voice that breaks them will command complete, anxious, and often critical attention. The able host gracefully inserts a gentle comment, a note of mild humor, into this void, relaxing her audience while encouraging a broader conversation that can comfortably split into subconversations again. With the party back on track, the host lets go of her reins of control, settling comfortably and gracefully into the background again.

Leading without leading in charrettes takes exactly this skill. The more subtle and artful this leadership, the less likely the group will be aware of it. Very few people are endowed with both the quietude for listening carefully and the courage to launch into dangerous silences. To become a facilitator who can lead without leading, practice and determination are required.

Rule 8. Move In, Move Out, Move Across

Rule 8 summarizes our solution to an unavoidable problem: Any charrette worth the effort will open up questions at many scales and across many issues. The broader the scale, and the more issues to be dealt with, the greater will be the need to examine these questions at the appropriate scale and with sufficient focus. Obviously charrette

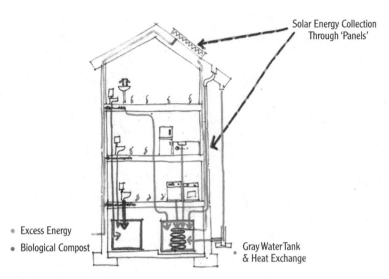

Solar Energy Collection
Through 'Panels'

• Excess Energy
• Biological Compost

Gray Water Tank
& Heat Exchange

Sustainable Design Components

Sample drawing from the "moving in" phase of the Sustainable Urban Landscapes, Brentwood Design Charrette, in which the energy and waste systems of a single building are examined.

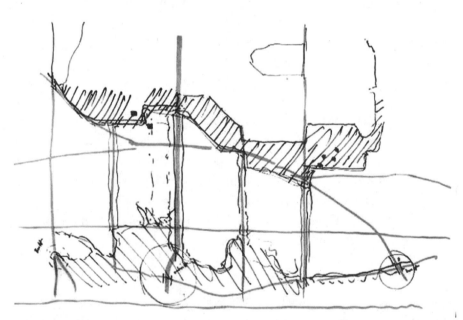

Sample drawing from the "moving out" phase of the Sustainable Urban Landscapes, Brentwood Design Charrette. In this case, ecological issues of water movement through buildings, streets, and the site are very rapidly examined at the scale of the whole 500-acre site.

organizers can divide up the team to deal with these different issues and scales: planners can deal with large-scale issues, architects can tackle small-scale issues, and engineers can focus on technical issues, with citizens and other stakeholders scattered around. Unfortunately, this is a recipe for dis-integrated design, in which no synergy between issues is unearthed, rendering the charrette process no better than the conventional models it presumes to replace.

What can be done? There is no way to completely eliminate the inevitable tension between the part and the whole. But it can be made a creative tension by *moving in*, to small-scale issues, *moving out*, to large-scale issues, and *moving across*, from one issue to another. How is this to be accomplished? We might start with a 2-hour initial meeting of the table of the whole to discuss the charrette program. This discussion could be followed by a 2-hour breakout session at four subcommittee tables, which might focus, for example, on energy use, transportation, green infrastructure, and housing. When time is up, the subcommittees would report back to the table of the whole with their findings, soliciting comments from the members of the other tables. Facilitators could bring to light points of connection and conflict between issue areas (for example, the need to orient buildings to the south for passive solar gain often conflicts with an equally compelling need to orient buildings to the east and west and north for community design reasons). It is precisely these points of conflict that eventually spawn compelling and holistic design solutions. Charrette leaders must therefore bring them to the attention of the group, identifying them as important charrette design challenges.

Rule 9. The Drawing Is a Contract

Rule 9 is very simple, so we can keep it brief. The fundamental purpose of all drawings produced is to embody the consensus arrived at by the charrette team. In this way, the drawings are like a contract, but in pictures rather than words. It is less important to fully resolve all design issues than it is to be sure that the drawings truly represent consensus. The drawings need not be pretty; it is the consensus that is beautiful. If the drawing is a contract, that must also mean that drawings cannot be substantively altered after the charrette without the consent of the team. Absent such consent, it can no longer be claimed that the drawings represent consensus, and they therefore no longer function for the purpose intended. This sense of the drawing as a contract, not breakable without the consent of the group, should be built into the memorandum of understanding between project sponsors and charrette organizers. It may take the form of an agreement to hold follow-up meetings with the charrette team members as the project approaches implementation or as small or large changes to the consensus design proposal are considered.

These nine rules collectively constitute both a methodology and an ethic for the charrette. Remembering all and adhering to them as closely as possible makes the complicated task of running a charrette much more manageable. They apply mostly to the charrette event itself but influence the workshops that precede the charrette, workshops that are discussed in the following chapter.

5. The Workshops

Charrettes are like a dance; they need to be choreographed. Within the choreography for any dance, there is much room for chance and a diversity of individual approaches. But choreography is the necessary armature that prevents diversity from degenerating into chaos; it stops a dance from devolving into staggers and stumbles. The first measures of this choreography in our practice are the *pre-charrette workshops*, defined here as long, multiparticipant meetings with some product outcome, such as an explicit design program or design brief for a site, as their goal. The workshops described below are crucial for implementation charrettes. They are less critical for visioning charrettes, and in some cases they can be eliminated entirely; instead, the design brief may be reviewed by an advisory committee made up of community representatives and business and political leaders. The discussion in this chapter, then, specifically applies to implementation charrettes and the workshop stages necessary to arrive at a robust consensus plan within them.

We typically schedule between two and four multi-hour workshops before the charrette event itself. Prior to more elaborate and lengthy charrettes, the following workshop events are important: the principles workshop, the goal and objectives workshop, the numerical requirements workshop, and the performance targets workshop. The minimum number of workshops would be two, in which case they would be a goal and objectives workshop and a numerical requirements/performance targets workshop. In such an abbreviated schedule, the discussion on principles would be folded into the goal and objectives workshop. The last workshop described below combines the numerical requirements and performance targets workshops into one final workshop. In certain cases in which the numerical requirements and performance targets are elaborate and crucial, and in which the stakeholder group is willing to commit the time and the budget allows, this workshop can be split into two different workshops.

The workshops have two main functions: first, to review, amend, and adopt the design brief for the charrette, and second, to begin the crucial social transformation of a group of separate stakeholders into a workable and working charrette team. In this way, the workshops also operate like the talk phase of the charrette described in chapter 4, functioning to overcome barriers between people and forge a working team, but in this case the team bonds not over the challenge of producing the design, but rather over the challenge of articulating its guiding framework.

Choosing Participants

Choosing the workshop participants is a crucial step. We do not see this as an entirely democratic process dominated by citizen volunteers or neighborhood residents (although they certainly have a role). We see it as a way to assemble the actors who would ordinarily be in a position to influence the project in such a way that they can work together toward a more favorable outcome. We find it useful to imagine stakeholders as falling into broad categories. A list of these categories might include the following:

- public safety officials (fire, police)
- transportation and transit authorities
- housing developers
- economic development officers
- nongovernmental organizations (NGOs) concerned with housing, environment, and transportation
- school district officials
- environmental regulators
- advocates for the elderly or impaired
- land and property owners in the district
- municipal planners and engineers
- elected officials
- cultural groups (historic preservation, arts)
- recreation groups (active and passive recreation)
- merchants from the area

Different charrettes might have slightly different lists depending on the site and the issues, but this list will give the reader a good idea of the range of stakeholder groups that might be involved. If 3 or 4 people come from each stakeholder category, you can easily end up with more than 50 people participating. We have managed workshops with close to 200 participants, but 30 to 60 participants is more the norm.

Sixty participants can be easily managed at the workshops, but that is too many to participate meaningfully in the charrette itself. Later in this chapter we will discuss the concept of the "outer table," where all stakeholders participate, and the "inner table," where only a more manageable and productive 15 or fewer stakeholders participate. Note that the pre-charrette workshops are open to a broad and potentially large group of invited stakeholders.

A charrette is an open process in which anyone who has a stake in the outcome should be at the table. That having been said, there are occasions when a particular person may not be well equipped to handle the intensely collaborative atmosphere of the charrette, or even the workshops. Most charrettes we have worked on have had one or two individuals who fit this profile. They must be accepted, respected, and worked with. On the other hand, in many of the communities we have worked in, people have self-selected, or have been proposed, for their known capacity to work productively and cordially with others. It is perfectly appropriate for charrette organizers to ask whether a potential participant can work well with others. Large organizations such as development firms or city engineering offices often have more than one high-level employee who could adequately represent them. Charrette organizers are well advised to ask whether a proposed participant is a good collaborator. If the answer is no, then another member of the team might be chosen in their stead.

Workshop 1: Principles Workshop

The principles workshop should be two to three hours long. It has two basic parts: the presentation and the roundtable discussions. The presentation is the organizers' first, and potentially most important, opportunity to provide participants with an overview of the main problems of the site and discuss the principles underlying sustainable communities. Very few participants will be familiar with these principles. The intimate relationship between land use and transportation, for example, will be almost entirely unknown to most of the stakeholders in the room. Somehow the organizers must present information that explains the intricate Gordian knot of the city and its systems in coherent form. The principles provide a useful way to deliver this information. If the principles are robust and accurately embody an insightful and higher-level synthesis of the problem, this initial presentation can provide a real chance for education. Conversely, the pictures and data presented can help reinforce those principles that are more easily understood. The PowerPoint presentation of design principles used at the Damascus Area Design Workshop can be viewed online at http://www.jtc.sala.ubc.ca/Damascus/Principles.htm.

The principles presentation can be as long as an hour. It must be delivered by someone who is a dynamic and engaging speaker and who knows the issues in depth. More important, the presenter must know how the issues connect to one another. The presentation must unpack those connections for stakeholders, most of whom will not have had occasion to ponder them.

The presentation should conclude with a question and answer period that encourages conversation and opinions from the assembled stakeholders. The question and answer period can be as long as a half hour and should be followed by a 20–30-minute break.

Breaks are important and should not be cut short if presentations or questions go long. Refreshment breaks keep participants happy and alert. More important, the

The presentation: The outer table gathers to review the goal and objectives at a pre-charrette workshop for the Maple Ridge Smart Growth on the Ground design charrette.

break is the only chance participants have for one-on-one conversations. A lot of the coming together of the group occurs during breaks.

The break should be followed by roundtable conversations of 6 to 10 persons, each managed by one design facilitator. The objective of these discussions is to review the written draft principles and revise them as necessary. We usually break out into tables that are stakeholder based, so that participants from related interest areas can approach the principles from a common perspective. There is a danger that this arrangement will produce narrow thinking, however, and if the occasion merits it, it can help to seed the tables with persons with a different perspective to maintain balance. It is particularly important to balance participants from the private and public sectors. One stakeholder from each table can be elected as the recorder. This person will be responsible for reporting to the larger group, leaving the facilitator free to carefully follow the conversation and direct it to a successful conclusion.

The principles workshop tends to be the most relaxed of the four workshops. With usually only one sheet of words to review, participants can take time to opine

Roundtable discussions: Smaller breakout tables discuss the goal and objectives for the Oliver, BC, charrette with a facilitator.

and philosophize without going irreversibly off task. This stage also allows the stake-holders to get to know one another better in a lower-risk context than later work-shops or the charrette itself. The project facilitators can use this workshop to gain the measure of the group and begin to understand who are the creative movers and who are the more conservative thinkers. Facilitators can also practice the art of find-ing commonality, suggesting language that satisfies all parties by employing facili-tation strategies such as, "It sounds like you are both saying X. What if we used a phrase like Y? Would that work?"

The product of this first workshop is an approved set of principles. The task becomes one of wordsmithing: crafting the language of the principles provided in draft form by the charrette organizers. I am always surprised at how many minor changes stakeholders can propose to a principle that I had thought perfect. Almost always, it becomes better in the process. With different tables working on the same principles, you will get more than one result for each principle. It is up to the facil-itators to synthesize all of these suggestions into one final statement. It is possible to make changes during the workshop on an image of the principles projected on a screen, typing in the changes as they are suggested. More frequently we ask the group to ponder the proposed changes and attempt to synthesize their suggestions in principles we then revise between workshops. This revision is endorsed at the beginning of the second workshop on goal and objectives. In our experience, the revisions are accepted if the facilitators have respected the spirit of the suggestions made. This process of adding nuance and detail to the principles makes them longer and potentially unwieldy. Thus we recommend that the organizers begin with very short principles, expecting them to lengthen during review.

If budgets are tight, or the project small, or for municipalities with an already appropriate set of principles, this workshop may not be necessary or may be com-bined with a subsequent workshop.

Workshop 2: Goal and Objectives Workshop

As discussed in chapter 3, principles are general and often lack direct formal impli-cations. In contrast, the goal and objectives begin the process of transforming prin-ciples into site-specific actions. The purpose of the goal and objectives workshop is to validate the site-specific goal and objectives before taking up the more direc-tive numerical requirements and performance targets at the workshop that follows.

The goal and objectives are not drafted at the workshop, but rather presented to the stakeholders as a carefully researched and footnoted draft. The footnotes should link the objectives to the policy documents that support them. It may be appropriate to review the goal and objectives with the project sponsors to ensure their comfort with them prior to the workshop; however, facilitators must be careful to honor their professional responsibility to the process if project sponsors (typically senior city staff) exert pressure for too much digression from policy or previously approved principles prior to the workshop.

The goal and objectives workshop should be three to four hours long. As in the principles workshop, we begin with a presentation, but this one is kept to a half hour and is used mostly to read through the objectives, with a few pictures used for illustration. It is difficult to make this presentation engaging, but the attempt must be made, and a dynamic speaker is again required. The goal and objectives presentation used at the Damascus Area Design Workshop can be viewed via the Web links provided in the appendix.

The bulk of the goal and objectives workshop is devoted to roundtable conversations of six to ten persons, with each table managed by a design facilitator. Each table is asked to review and suggest revisions to the draft goal and objectives. Again, one stakeholder from each table can be elected as the recorder, who will be responsible for reporting to the larger group. These tables should be occupied by the same groups of stakeholders as at the previous principles workshop. Although there might be some advantage in shifting the composition of tables between workshops, we believe it is important to keep the tables largely the same. The tables will be asked to elect one or two of their members to represent them at the charrette, and they need time to take the measure of the man or woman who might represent them.

The time allotted to roundtable conversations should be broken into three roughly equal parts: first the goal is discussed, then the first half of the objectives are tackled, and finally the last half of the objectives are reviewed and amended. There are two reporting sessions: the first for the goal statement, and another at the end of the workshop for the objectives.

The goal and objectives workshop is more arduous than the principles workshop. Stakeholders have to cover more ground and have less opportunity or occasion to philosophize. Facilitators must be skillful at keeping the group engaged and must ensure that no stakeholders tire to the point of holding back from participation. Facilitators must methodically and enthusiastically make progress toward consensus. Occasionally there will be two or more ideas for a change that cannot, because of their complexity, all be easily integrated into the statement. In such cases, the facilitator must ask permission from the group to take their input under advisement for further reflection after the session, with results to be presented later. Most stake-holders are prepared to allow this.

At this workshop, stakeholders are getting to know one another and their facil-itators better and becoming accustomed to coming to consensus quickly. Both of these changes are important to the eventual success of the charrette and thus should be acknowledged as a crucial, albeit not immediately apparent, outcome of this workshop.

In this spirit, and given the difficulty of the task, we recommend taking many breaks—three or four during the workshop. As mentioned before, breaks keep par-ticipants fresh and allow them to have one-on-one conversations. They should not be shortened if work sessions go long.

As in the principles workshop, facilitators should expect many changes to the language of the goal and objectives, but very few complete deletions or exotic addi-tions. This is because the goal and objectives, like everything else in the charrette, are grounded in policy. Stakeholders understand this and know instinctively that this grounding must be respected; they understand that any changes suggested must fit within the policy framework.

There will probably be changes proposed by stakeholders that will need to be discussed with the entire group and approved before the workshop ends. Good facil-itators can capture the areas of strong agreement, however, and try to express these to the group at the end of the session. Similarly, the facilitator can identify areas of disagreement that have emerged. These areas of disagreement can remain "issues outstanding." In this case, the facilitators can request permission from the group to ponder the areas of disagreement after the workshop and to craft goal and objec-tives language to resolve the outstanding issues. These revisions can be reviewed and approved at the beginning of the next workshop.

The goal and objectives workshop is fundamental to the charrette process and cannot be eliminated for any reason. Better to shortchange expert support for the charrette itself than to eliminate this step. Goals and objectives promulgated at the charrette can often have a lasting value in guiding development, even if the design produced at the charrette is never adopted as policy.

Workshop 3: Numerical Requirements and Performance Targets Workshop

The products of the goal and objectives workshop establish the foundation for the charrette design brief. The numerical requirements and performance targets spec-ify the tasks to be accomplished at the charrette. They grow directly out of the objectives, are supported by research, and do not contradict the imperatives in the policy base. A workshop must be conducted to amend and validate these crucial requirements and targets.

The numerical requirements and performance targets workshop should be four hours long. As in the previous workshops, the facilitators present a draft numerical requirements and performance targets document to the group. This draft depends heavily on the language approved in the previous goal and objectives workshop. Everything included in the requirements and targets draft must be tied back to the goal and objectives, as well as to the research and policy base that validates them. As the sample design briefs provided via Web links in the appendix show, virtually all inclusions are referenced to research or policy documents.

Unless the draft requirements and targets document is blessedly brief (say, fewer than 1,000 words), it is usually not advisable to start the session by presenting the entire document. It would be impossibly dull if one tried to read and explain every word of the draft. However, an overview of the central themes and the most important requirements in the draft will help get the day rolling. Remember that participants are likely to be unfamiliar with the content of the document even if it was distributed prior to the meeting. Orientation to the material should be confined to less than 45 minutes. The bulk of the time for this workshop should then be devoted to roundtable discussions, first to deal with the numerical requirements, then to review and amend the performance targets.

The group should be broken into the same stakeholder-based tables used in the previous workshops. Again, one stakeholder at each table is elected as the recorder. In most cases, it is advisable to divide the tasks of reviewing the draft among the different tables, with business interests, for example, focusing on economic development and commercial requirements first while environmental regulators review the green infrastructure performance targets and open space requirements first. When each table has satisfactorily completed "its own area," it moves on to the other issues. Again, there is a danger in this strategy. Tables made up of individuals from similar stakeholder categories might interpret the document too narrowly, ignoring other issue areas in favor of their own. This risk is mitigated by the fact that the goal and objectives were arrived at through collaboration by the whole group and still hold overall sway. In addition, the draft document has already been carefully elaborated by the charrette facilitators and presumably reflects an overall balance between issue areas. Tables should be required to finish their own issue areas in time to take on at least some of the other issue areas. This strategy will prevent collective and individual silo thinking by forcing at least two sets of eyes to examine issues from alternative perspectives.

The objective for each table is to review, amend, and endorse the numerical requirements and performance targets of the design brief. These requirements and targets can be controversial. As discussed in chapter 3, seemingly mundane issues such as parking requirements are in fact the sine qua non of sprawl. Debates on density and parking requirements can be heated. The most important tools facilitators have in guiding these debates toward consensus are the results of the previous workshops. If one of the objectives is to provide walkable communities with commercial services and transit within a 5-minute walk of all residents, then facilitators can remind participants of their support for this objective and of the research indicating that this objective cannot be achieved if most of the landscape is consumed by roadways and parking lots serving low-density single-family homes. It is possible that consensus will break down at this point, with participants realizing, perhaps for the first time, that the changes to the status quo needed to achieve their objective are too dramatic. More frequently, this becomes an occasion for stakeholders to understand for the first time how land use, transportation, parking policy, and density issues all interact, and to realize that solutions need to be holistic if there is to be any hope of their being effective. Again, we can see that these workshops have a value that extends beyond the simple pragmatic necessity of approving a design brief. They are problem-based educational opportunities for the very people presently creating unsustainable auto-oriented landscapes.

This workshop is intense for both facilitators and stakeholders. It should be broken up with three breaks of at least 20 minutes. This means that there will be four discussion sessions, probably two on the numerical requirements and two on the performance targets. Again, the purpose of the breaks is both to refresh the participants and to encourage one-on-one conversations among them. By this workshop, there should be more than a few conversations between stakeholders who previously didn't know one another and who came from very different political and economic positions in relation to urban development.

It is unlikely that this workshop will generate a final approved design brief with every word endorsed—there will be too many different tables proposing too many different changes to the same items. The facilitators must again ask the stakeholders to allow them to amend the draft immediately after the workshop. If significant disagreement exists on certain points, then compromise language must be circulated and approved prior to the charrette. It is conceivable that disagreement on the requirements and targets could remain by the first day of the charrette, although this has not happened to us to date. If it did, we would either hold an additional short workshop a week or two prior to the charrette to iron it out or devote a portion of the first session of the charrette to arriving at a compromise.

Good facilitation at this last workshop is crucial. The facilitators must gently keep the stakeholders focused, elicit comments from the more reserved, limit the talk time of the more verbose, actively search for areas of consensus in the white noise of apparent disagreement, and be sure that the clock remains your friend.

The breaks are probably most crucial for the facilitators. In addition to providing them with a chance to relax after the stress of group facilitation, the breaks provide an opportunity for them to check in with one another, ensuring that the work is getting done at other tables and adjusting strategies on the fly to be sure that the group as a whole "gets to yes."

By this session, the stakeholders will know the others at their table very well. At the end of the workshop, each table must elect or choose delegates to represent them at the charrette if the total number of stakeholder participants is more than twenty. In other words, stakeholders from this larger group, sometimes called the "outer table," must select stakeholders to represent them at the collaborative design charrette table, called the "inner table." Depending on numbers, each table will elect one or two of its members to represent them, such that the stakeholders at the inner table number between ten and fifteen. Larger numbers are possible if the charrette will clearly divide into discrete geographic areas, or if for some reason it has been decided that the charrette should produce more than one scheme (commonly the case for visioning charrettes, for example). Occasionally stakeholders who are nominated will decline. More often they will consider it an honor, even though the time requirement can be onerous. These groups generally tend to choose the person who they believe can best represent their interests. Once in a while, they choose a person who is less than diplomatic. More often, they instinctively understand that diplomacy and a capacity to work with others are the best tools for ensuring that their interests are protected, and they choose accordingly.

Obviously, this numerical requirements and performance targets workshop cannot be eliminated. In our view, it is impossible to conduct a meaningful charrette without a carefully drafted design brief, and the requirements and targets section is the heart of the design brief. Like the goal and objectives, the numerical requirements and performance targets can sometimes be more influential than the design outcomes they presumably are a mere vehicle for. Conversations that revolve around the design brief often resonate years later, as was the case in Surrey, where the East Clayton sustainable community design charrette eventually led to a citywide bylaw change allowing secondary suites anywhere in the city.

Some examples of completed design briefs are available for review via the Web links in the appendix. You will note that although they are all very different, they all conform to the guidelines provided above.

6. The Charrette

This chapter describes how to conduct a charrette. Rather than providing an exhaustive, and in many aspects repetitive, description of the various possible charrette types and patterns, I first describe a four-day implementation charrette in detail, then discuss variations on this prototypical charrette—longer, shorter, visioning, implementation, and so forth—at the chapter's end.

Planning the Charrette

The longest charrette we have ever done was eight days; the shortest was three days. Our most common pattern is the four-day charrette, spanning Thursday to Tuesday, with stakeholders getting Saturday and Sunday off. This length is a compromise between our belief that the charrette should be longer and the difficulty of getting the right stakeholders to commit more than four partial days to the process. Our partial-day format, with stakeholders on hand from 9:00 A.M. TO 1:00 or 2:00 P.M., also allows designer-only time to move the process forward expeditiously on three of the days.

If the principles, goal, objectives, numerical requirements, and performance targets generated in the pre-charrette workshops are robust, and if all participants are committed to them, the charrette process described below should unfold smoothly in the time allowed. The workshops are designed to resolve potentially divisive issues ahead of time. If you have done well in the first steps, the design proposal should, in a real way, unfold almost by itself, making the experience all that much more miraculous to the participants. We therefore cannot overemphasize the value of the pre-charrette workshops and how important it is that they be tied to existing local, regional, and national policies (see chapter 5).

Inner and Outer Table

The prototypical four-day charrette has an inner and outer table of stakeholder participants. As discussed previously, the *outer table* comprises all the individuals who participated in the pre-charrette workshops. The *inner table* is the smaller group of individuals who will participate in the charrette itself, drawn from the members of the outer table. In certain cases, the group that worked on the design brief is small enough that all of its members can be at the charrette table, and in this case there is no inner and outer table. A very focused charrette, such as one for a new light rail line down one street, at which a narrower than usual group of participants is required, may not require an inner and outer table. Finally, visioning charrettes don't need an outer table because the participants are largely designers working to a brief produced by others.

Presence or Absence of Elected Officials

Should elected officials participate in charrettes? This might seem like a simple question. If an elected official is in a position to rule on a project, he or she should most certainly be involved in the charrette at which that project is designed. Elected city councillors have been very strong members of our charrette teams. They are typically horizontal thinkers who understand how economic and political dimensions connect. On the other hand, city councillors and mayors are often called upon to adjudicate and give final approval to development proposals and zoning changes. There are legitimate concerns in some quarters about the potential perception of conflict of interest if city councillors find themselves acting as both proponents and adjudicators of the charrette proposal. We have found no clear and universally applicable rule to govern this situation, and we usually defer to the legal and political opinions of our municipal sponsors.

Basic Resources Needed for a Charrette

Space

Over the years we have considered and tried various locations for charrettes—school sites, university design studios, the basement of city hall, and many other venues. Now we usually use hotel conference rooms. There are a number of simple reasons for this seemingly unimaginative choice: These spaces are set up for meetings and are usually quite flexible. Hotels usually provide catering services on site, not to mention accommodations for visiting facilitators. Additional rooms can be rented for meetings, storage, production, and so forth. We do have *some* standards, however:

we demand windows. Four days of designing in the typically windowless hotel conference room sucks the energy out of even the most well-organized charrette. Financial considerations may lead organizers to place all the participants in one room. This can work for small charrettes with fewer than ten participants, but more than that requires more rooms for breakout tables or subteam work. Most hotel conference facilities have many different-sized rooms or rooms that can be subdivided with soundproof partitions. Happily, most hotels now have easy wireless connections to the Internet; this is a must.

Materials

The essential material for a charrette is tracing paper and lots of it. It comes in rolls ranging from 8 inches to 4 feet wide. We prefer the thinnest of tracing papers, usually buff in color. Some tracing paper is almost opaque, which frustrates any attempt to put more than a couple of layers on top of one another and still see the base map below. Layering trace over trace assists in the collaborative process, allowing the participants' conversations to be reflected in the increasingly sophisticated iterations of the concept drawn there.

We equip charrette kit boxes with a host of drawing implements and a limited selection of drafting tools. Our marking tools range from the thinnest of black pens and pencils to wide colored markers. The advent of computer graphics has made graphic design markers a bit harder to find, and they are still quite expensive. We limit the palette of marker colors in the kit to control costs as well as to ensure that the colors will be compatible and that drawings from one group are likely to have the same colors showing as drawings from another group. Using water-soluble black inks (as in Pilot or Flair pens) on tracing paper in combination with permanent colored markers is an especially good strategy. Colored marker can be "erased" from the tracing paper without removing the black lines by coloring over with a lighter-colored marker the area you want removed and wiping off with tissue before the marker medium dries.

We also make extensive use of colored pencil sets available at art stores. Colored pencils are more affordable than markers but don't replace them. Finally, and perhaps surprisingly, we have started to make great use of correction fluid, sometimes known as "whiteout." Computers have also made this old mainstay of office life a bit harder to find, but it is excellent material for painting directly onto aerial photo base maps, obviating the need to redraw portions of the site context that are not proposed for change.

We also include a few basic drafting tools such as scales, triangles, and parallel rules. Surprisingly, these tools are less crucial than one might suppose. Skilled

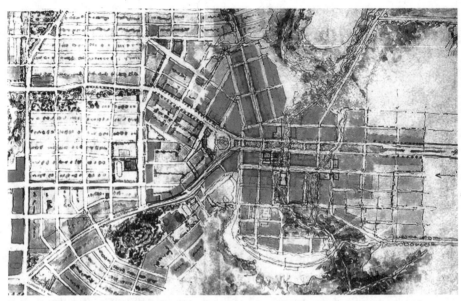

Example of a final plan drawing from the Damascus Area Design Workshop, drawn with water-soluble black pen and permanent colored design markers on buff tracing paper. The colors can be erased if changes are desired. The markers can be used on tracing paper to get watercolor-like effects, as shown here in the vegetated areas. This very forgiving method is easy to teach to nondesigner members of the team; thus the final plan can be worked on by many hands at once. Our thanks to Rob Lane of the Regional Plan Association for teaching us this method.

designers can draw to scale on the aerial photo without tools, with only an occasional use of the scale to be sure they are controlling sizes correctly.

Computers are crucial in charrettes for a number of reasons. Photo visualizations, PowerPoint shows, and quick SketchUp-style diagrams are increasingly produced at our charrettes. It goes without saying that the text of the charrette proposal will be written on a computer. Many participants are now bringing their own laptops to charrettes, which should be encouraged. Organizers should guarantee that there will be enough computers on hand to ensure a ratio of no less than one computer per five participants.

Finally, we ask that design facilitators bring their own favorite drawing tools. Most skilled design facilitators have their own favorite way of doing drawings, and it makes no sense to try to supply each of them with their favorite implements.

Budgets

Budgets for charrettes vary with differences in project scope or staffing. Our four-day prototypical charrette might have a rough budget, in U.S. dollars, as seen in table 6.1.

Detail from a final plan drawing from the Damascus Area Design Workshop, drawn with black water-soluble fine-tip pen, colored pencils, and correction fluid (a.k.a. whiteout, used for roads) painted directly on an aerial photo base sheet on bond paper. This technique is also easy to teach others on the team who are not designers or are unfamiliar with it. Our thanks to Warren Byrd of Nelson Byrd Woltz for teaching us this method.

Some readers will undoubtedly think this is impossibly expensive. It is not. It's what it takes to do the job correctly. It is also instructive to remember that when development takes place, municipalities typically spend many times more than this amount on the engineering studies required for sewer and transportation infrastructure alone, not including separate studies on environmental mitigation and economic development opportunities. Those studies start from the assumption that existing patterns of sprawl will be continued and thus represent part of the problem, not part of the solution; far better to spend a fraction of that amount on a design charrette.

Staffing

Trained staff are needed to manage, facilitate, support, and record the workshops and charrette. A staff-to-participant ratio of about 1:6 should be the target. Design facilitators must be able to facilitate conversations, be at least moderately good designers, be able to organize groups to meet their goals, and be generally nice people to work

Table 6.1

Food		
Workshops	150 coffee services @ $10	$2,000
Charrette	240 meal services @ $40	$9,600
Guest facilitators	4 @ $6,000	$24,000
Materials	Paper, pens, photography, reproduction	$5,000
Transportation	Travel costs for facilitators: airline, bus, rental car, etc.	$3,000
Staff time	Three workshops staffing	$9,600
	Three workshops prep time	$16,000
	Charrette prep time	$12,000
	Staff at charrette	$16,000
	Final report (concept not implementation)	$14,000
	Implementation follow-up	$20,000
Total		$131,200

with. Our design facilitators are drawn from the design and planning professions, and that is what we recommend.

The Opening Event

The typical charrette begins with a kickoff event, usually open to a wide range of invited stakeholders and other interested parties. The "outer table" stakeholders from the pre-charrette workshops would most certainly be in attendance, as would any of their colleagues who could not participate in those workshops with them. We often invite the broader public as well to widen the influence of the process and add another layer of input for the team.

Ordinarily the opening event has two parts. The first part is an organized presentation of the project, the problem, and the site. This presentation can most appropriately be given by charrette staff or possibly by key staff from sponsoring agencies (such as the director of planning for the host municipality). Plenty of maps and site photographs should be projected on a screen for the large crowd as well as displayed on the walls for more careful review. The principles, goal, and objectives in the design brief provide the organizational framework for the presentation, and they should be supplemented with an overview of the most crucial

Opening events provide a chance for luminaries and key stakeholders to weigh in, as well as for the charrette organizers to repeat and reinforce fundamental design principles for the whole group.

and challenging numerical requirements and performance targets. This presentation should be 20 minutes to a half hour in length. Even though most attendees will have heard the principles, goal, and objectives more than once, is worth the time to repeat them now. The more often they are said aloud, the better they will be integrated into the thinking of the participants. In our experience, it takes a certain amount of time, and insistent repetition, before participants can use them to "frame" the problem. Once they have integrated the design principles, they will see the world and its problems in new ways. What was seen as a parking and traffic problem can now can be framed as the problem of organizing land uses so that everyone is "within a 5-minute walk of commercial services and transit."[1]

The second part of the opening event is devoted to individual presentations by stakeholders, each of whom presents their own personal take on the problem. A typical lineup would include the mayor of the host city, the head of the development community, the head of the local stream stewardship committee, the head of the regional transit authority, and three or four others, each of whom would

Model implementation charrette schedule

DAY 1 THURSDAY	Activity	Sub-activity	Participants
	Opening event		"Inner table" and "outer table;" invited stakeholders; invited technical experts
	Bus tour		Inner table, invited stakeholders and elected officials; invited technical experts
	Lunch		Everyone who was on the bus
	First Design session	Discussion over the big map	First design meeting of inner table
		Break out into issue areas	Inner table
		Short break	Inner table
		Reporting session and adjournment	Inner table
	Designer-only time	Facilitator meeting	Facilitators

DAY 2 FRIDAY	Activity	Sub-activity	Participants
	Coffee and talk		Inner table
	Second design session	Report on progress and discuss tasks	Inner table
		Breakout sessions	
		Break	

Time in schedule	Event duration	Comments	Phase
8:30–10:00	1.5 hr	Coffee, rolls, fruit, and cheese	TALK
10:00–12:00	2 hr	School bus required	
12:00–1:00	1 hr	Catered sit-down meal. Speakers on technical issues possible.	
1:00–2:15	1.25 hr	Everyone gets to say their piece. First ideas floated. Precedents possible introduced.	
2:30–4:00	1.5 hr	Technical focus tied to performance targets in the design brief. Question forms may be provided to facilitators	
4:15	15 min	Coffee, cookies, fruit, cheese	
4:15–5:00	45 min	Facilitators identify areas of conflict and synergy	
5:00–5:30	30 min	Discuss progress, personality issues, complexities of the design problem that only now emerge, facilitation techniques	

Time in schedule	Event duration	Comments	Phase
8:30–9:00	30 min	Let it go long if it seems wise	
9:00–9:10	10 min	Facilitators can provide sense of where they think there is consensus and what the tasks for the morning might be	TALK
9:10–11:00	2 hr	Different charrettes might have different ways of breaking this out. One way is by mixing the groups from the previous day and assigning them geographic areas at a variety of scales, with synthesis of previously examined issues identified	TALK/ DOODLE
11:00–11:20		Refreshed coffee table same as arrival	

Model implementation charrette schedule

DAY 2 (cont.) FRIDAY	Activity	Sub-activity	Participants
		Reporting session	
	Lunch		
	Third design session	Return to breakout sessions	
	Designer-only time	Facilitator meeting	Facilitators
		Facilitator work time	Facilitators

DAY 3 MONDAY	Activity	Sub-activity	Participants
	Mid course corrections		Inner table, outer table key elected officials; high level staff, high level trade representitives, NGO representitives
	Review results of midcourse correction		Inner table

Time in schedule	Event duration	Comments	Phase
11:20–12:15	45 min	Facilitators can identify areas of synergy that seem to be emerging and probe the participants for their impressions of the practicality and efficacy of emerging strategies based on both their hopes and their real-world experience	
12:15–1:15	1 hr	A full hour is needed for lunch. Buffet lunch such as wraps and sandwiches, cut-up vegetables, fruits, desserts, soup, tea, coffee and soft drinks	
1:15–2:30	1.25 hr	Back to work in same groups. Carry forward design ideas based on reporting session before lunch	DOODLE
2:30–3:00	30 min	Facilitators discuss progress and areas of continued concern; identify objectives that are being met and those that are not; identify team personality issues and strategies for overcoming; decide what drawings to clean up and present at midcourse correction tomorrow AM	
3:00–5:30	2.5 hr	Complete unfinished diagrams	

Time in schedule	Event duration	Comments	Phase
9:00–11:00	2 hr	Pinup presentation in the charrette room or rooms. Presentations made by stakeholders as much as possible. Presentations focus on this question: do these ideas meet the agreed-upon objectives of the project? Leave half the time for back-and-forth. Depending on group size, organize discussion tables no larger than twelve persons. Save time for reporting from tables and recording results. Essential question: do you feel comfortable enough with what you see to endorse it going forward?" Coffee and muffins for possibly large crowd required.	DOODLE
11:00–12:00	1 hr	Facilitators move the discussion to more concrete approvals. Gain consensus on specific design ideas to be executed in the fast-approaching "draw" phase of the charrette. Discuss how the emerging design achieves the objectives and identify gaps if any.	DOODLE/ DRAW

Model implementation charrette schedule

DAY 3 (cont.) MONDAY	Activity	Sub-activity	Participants
	Lunch		
	Third design session		
	Designer-only time	Facilitators meeting	Facilitators
		Facilitator draw session	Facilitators
DAY 4 TUESDAY	**Activity**	**Sub-activity**	**Participants**
	Coffee and talk		Inner table
	Final group meeting		
	Final design session	Morning	
		Lunch	
		Afternoon	

Time in schedule	Event duration	Comments	Phase
12:00–1:00	1 hr	Similar but not exactly the same menu as day before	
1:00–2:30	1.5 hr	This is when the transition to the draw phase occurs. A team can be assembled to work on the master plan and others to work on subareas or certain detail concepts, such as green streets or housing massing and use options. Tasks should relate directly to the charrette objectives and be oriented to finishing the items on the required products list in the design brief	DRAW
2:30–3:00	30 min	Final meeting of facilitators. Important to decide what can be reasonably finished and what time, if any, still needs to be devoted to negotiating alternatives if consensus is not complete	
3:00–5:30	2.5 hr	Facilitators work alone to move drawings from the morning forward	

Time in schedule	Event duration	Comments	Phase
8:30–9:00	30 min	Same as Friday but alter selections	
9:00–10:00	1 hr	This may seem like a lot of time on the last day of production, but this is the last chance to certify that the group is in true consensus, and if not, to develop strategies for dealing with this. Head facilitator should go through the issue areas and check in with stakeholders, looking for head-nodding consent to all the key decisions. Ask out loud, "should we move forward with the drawings?"	DRAW
10:00–12:00	2 hr	Work session. Facilitators shift into either production mode or making sure technical glitches are smoothed. Head facilitator makes sure subteams are functional and appropriately staffed.	
12:00		Lunch brought in and set out for working lunch	
12:00–2:00	2 hr	Stakeholders finish writing tasks for report and participate in drawing tasks as appropriate and as ability allows	

Model implementation charrette schedule

DAY 4 (cont.) TUESDAY	Activity	Sub-activity	Participants
	Designer-only time	Check-in	Facilitators
		Work time	
		Dinner	
	Presentation	Introductions	Inner table, outer table, key elected officials, high-level staff, high-level industry representatives, NGO representatives, interested public
		Proposals	
		Panel response	
		Comments and questions from the floor	

Time in	Event schedule	Comments duration	Phase
2:00–2:15	15 min	Last chance to coordinate drawings or shift production support to achieve list of required products	
2:15–5:30	3.25 hr	Facilitator work session with some stakeholders and staff photographing and scanning drawings to go into preformatted Power-Point template. Text of reports written. Key bullet points and phrases added to PowerPoint	
5:30–6:30	1 hr	Working dinner. As drawings are finished, facilitators can relax while staff make sure that PowerPoint comes together. One or more stakeholders are present to participate in production of slide show and prepare to present it	DEADLINE
7:00–7:30	30 min	Allow time to introduce problem, purpose of event, and give dignitaries time to provide comments. Provide coffee, tea, soft drinks, and cookies	
7:30–8:30	1 hr	Difficult to put all this in one hour, but any longer and the audience simply cannot absorb any more	
8:30–9:00	30 min	Panel of respected professionals and citizens responds to what they see, responding in 5-minute statements. Moderator can ask questions or ask panelists to give follow-up responses to the comments of other panel members as time allows	
9:00–9:20	20 min	Comments from the floor. Use microphones set in aisles or portable mikes. Moderator must be experienced to manage selecting speakers fairly and cutting off the long-winded delicately	

ideally talk for 5 minutes. This presentation too might seem redundant to those who have spent days in the pre-charrette workshops, covering these same perspectives and ensuring that they were amply represented in the design brief. But repetition is the soul of retention. In addition, this presentation allows high-level elected officials, municipal department heads, and corporate CEOs—people too busy to participate in all of the workshops—a chance to contribute to the process efficiently. The presence of these individuals at the opening event lends credibility to the charrette process in addition to making it that much more likely that these same officials will support the outcome. Finally, this high-level kickoff tends to fire up the members of the inner table, reinforcing a sense that the proposals they put forth will be implemented.

This and all other events must be catered. Catering is a major charrette expense that must be anticipated. Coffee and muffins can cost $10 per person, lunch $25, dinner $35 to $40. Catering costs for the larger events can be in the thousands of dollars each.

The Site Tour

The site tour is an important part of every charrette. Many of the stakeholders are familiar with the site, and for them it might seem unnecessary, but the site tour is a valuable way to consolidate the group into a team. For most charrettes, travel by bus is the only option, and the bus must be large enough accommodate the inner table, facilitators, staff, and invited guests and speakers. Only a bus allows organizers, sponsors, and guests to provide a running commentary on what is being seen outside the windows as it rolls by. Ideally, the speakers from the opening event will also speak during the site tour. Thus they can reiterate and demonstrate the points made in their earlier talk. The bus should roll to a halt at three to six key locations for 15-minute walks and talks. The value of these stops is much enhanced if one of the guests or stakeholders is prepared to explain the issues intrinsic to each location, such as traffic congestion, failing sewer mains, a new transit line, lack of affordable housing, parking problems, or stream degradation, to name a few. The tour should consume one and a half to two and a half hours, depending on the site and its complexity. Ideally, both the opening event and the bus tour would occur in the morning of the first day of the charrette, allowing participants to return to the charrette site in time for lunch.

This first lunch should be a sit-down meal. Good and healthy food is important for maintaining the morale of the group. On the last day, a buffet with sandwiches that can be brought back to work sessions would be appropriate, but not at this first important lunch.

Bus tours are an effective way for the participants to both see the real site and come together as a team. Various stakeholders and officials can discuss key locations in situ and explain the issues that pertain there.

A portion of the lunch hour can be devoted to a question and answer session. If technical experts have been brought in from outside the region, they might use this time to demonstrate their successful solutions for similar problems. Technical briefings—for example, on the impacts of storm drainage on receiving streams or on the status of downtown revitalization efforts—can be provided at this time. These presentations might summarize information drawn from the technical bulletins described in chapter 4.

The First Design Stage: Talk

Step One: Surrounding the Big Map

The first "design session" will be dominated by talk. It is here that the group confronts the "blank sheet" of the site. Facilitators can begin a conversation around the big map in all its blankness by asking each of the stakeholders for their ideas, reminding them that the objective is to conform to the principles, achieve the goal, and reach all of the objectives of the charrette. A large piece of transparent tracing paper might be rolled over the base map to make it less threatening for stakeholders to mark it—not with design solutions at this point, but at locations that in their view must be addressed. This is also the point at which stakeholders can safely state their nonnegotiable positions. Some of these positions are obvious: developers will say they can't do a project if it will lose money, politicians and senior staff will say they can't approve the project if there is no clear community benefit, natural resource regulators will say they can't sign off on a project that violates their mandate, and so forth. It's all been said before in the workshops, but it all bears restating. Facilitators can reassure the group that these objectives, which presumably are all articulated in the design brief, are not mutually exclusive. On the contrary, the emphasis should be on the synergies between them: for example, "a project that makes money and adds value to the community" while "providing capital necessary to restore the nearby stream" is how the facilitator might initially describe the desired results.

Facilitators might also ask participants how much they want to depart from status quo development patterns. In my experience, most stakeholders opt to depart from them quite markedly—which is surprising in light of the fact that most of them are typically in the business of replicating status quo development patterns every day! How can this be explained? Perhaps the very same people who are creating sprawl recognize its problems, yet feel individually powerless to do anything about it. It seems that the charrette process provides them with a means to break out of the suburban development paralysis of which they are also victims.

Finally, this might be the best time to discuss local or distant precedents that may be relevant. If you are fortunate enough to have good urban design examples in your region, those examples might be referenced. Certain projects tend to be universally liked. Others tend to be universally disliked. It's often hard to put your finger on exactly why. Using well-liked precedents as the basis for conversation gets to the other side of what might otherwise be lengthy, abstract, and potentially fruitless conversations about what features constitute quality. Stakeholders can quickly say, "I like that! Will it work on our site?" Facilitators can quickly draw a scale overlay of the precedent on the subject site, thus equipping participants with the visual language necessary for critical evaluations early on in the process. Charrette organizers can assemble these examples fairly easily by photographing local projects and providing the photos on display boards alongside aerial photos from Google Earth or locally available orthographic aerial photos (called "orthophotos," meaning that they have a uniform scale and can be measured from). If this is not possible, or if the budget doesn't allow it, various model projects and their densities are available online, notably at the Web sites of the Design Centre for Sustainability at the University of British Columbia, the Lincoln Institute of Land Policy, and 1000 Friends of Oregon.[2]

Step Two: Breakout Tables

There will come a point, after an hour or two at the big table, when the issues have all been unpacked, everyone's opinions voiced, and precedents assessed. It's time to move on. It is not practical for up to twenty people to start drawing on the big map at this time, so we take this occasion to move to smaller breakout tables to explore the problem in a more issue-focused way. At our charrettes, we typically form tables to explore general topics such as movement systems for cars, transit, and pedestrians; community systems for housing, jobs, and community services; green infrastructure systems for streams, riparian zones, storm drainage, parks, and boulevards; and energy systems for buildings and districts. Employment or housing issues might merit their own focused tables as well. The final list of tables will depend on the goal and objectives of the charrette and should reflect the organization and hierarchy that is expressed in the design brief.

Each breakout table should include one or more of the project facilitators. Their mission should be derived from the design brief. If one of the performance targets in the design brief, for example, is "reduce energy consumed by buildings by 60 percent," some options for doing just that should be discussed. Another table might propose strategies to reduce auto dependence by the 40 percent called for in the brief. It may be useful, especially when working with inexperienced facilitators, to provide them with questions on a worksheet ahead of time, complete with spaces for answers and diagrams.

We often provide plans at various scales for this phase. The charrette base map might be 4 x 6 feet—perfect for the final illustrative plan, but impossibly large for an examination of a district-scale transportation issue. For those larger-scale examinations, a sheet that is 12 x 18 inches (at a scale of 1:2,000 or 1:5,000, depending on site size) is best. Participants can quickly assess various circulation options on such small sheets. Conversely, the large base map is too small for an exploration of green street options or anything else at the parcel, street, or block scale. For these explorations, plans at a scale of 1:200 to 1:500 are more suitable.

Step Three: Bringing the Big Table Back

The table of the whole is reconvened after no more than an hour and a half. Each break-out table reports on its conclusions to the larger group and then entertains questions. Facilitators must be watchful for contradictions between the conclusions of one group and the conclusions of another. For example, a green table may say that impervious surfaces must be dramatically reduced, while a community table may suggest minimum densities for housing of a type that will cover more than 50 percent of the surface with pavement and rooftops. It is here that some synthetic options might be discovered, such as rethinking assumptions about the direct correlation between pavement and stream degradation (there isn't one—it's not the pavement or rooftop that's the problem; it's what happens to the water after it comes off the roof or pavement that is the problem!).

By this point, you have probably come to the end of the first day—a day well spent. Tomorrow will bring more talk and the beginning of the doodle phase.

The Second Design Stage: Talk to Doodle

The second day begins early, but we let people talk for a while before starting work. Muffins and coffee arrive before the participants, naturally facilitating informal conversation when they arrive. The participants are usually jazzed up with ideas after their nocturnal reflections on the first day, and they are anxious to share ideas and thoughts in informal one-on-one or small group conversations.

Eventually we reconvene the table of the whole. The facilitators might call for a short "check-in," asking participants to share their reflections on the first day and their hopes for the days ahead. The lack of obvious progress at this stage might cause anxiety for some, but the charrette organizers can allay those concerns.

There are variations on the next stage of a typical charrette. In the scenario described below, the group again breaks into smaller tables—but this time the tables focus on different areas of the site, not on different general issues. Alternative scenarios might include having teams continue to work on issues, but with cross-communication between teams enhanced through redistributing members; or having teams work on specific technical issues such as building reuse opportunities, downtown revitalization strategies, parking questions, or green street sections . At the other end of the scale, organizers might choose this time to have breakout tables generate "big ideas" for the whole site for later comparison and debate.

There are many alternatives, but after having tried many, we usually begin with issue-focused breakout tables that narrow the scope of examination and then expand

Facilitators must use drawing as a means to advance communication, not to depict their own idea of the "solution." An ability to draw and talk at the same time is helpful, but doing so is exceedingly difficult in practice.

out to synthesize the issues at a geographic scale in the next breakout session. In this scenario, we ensure that at least one member from each of the previous issue-focused tables is at each of the new breakout tables. Dividing the site geographically can be as simple as cutting up the big base map into four equal quadrants or, conversely, focusing more narrowly on three or four prototypical parts of the site, locations that might provide generalizable solutions for the whole.

By now it is appropriate to put marks that symbolize tentative proposals on the blank sheet. Expert facilitation by skilled designers is required. Design facilitation is different from dialogue facilitation. It's done with talk and a pencil: "We could do this or we could do that" (facilitator draws). "It could go here or go there" (marks the page). "It can be this high or this wide" (quickly generates an axonometric). "Where do *you* think it should go?" (hands the pencil to a stakeholder).

The skilled design facilitator is constantly listening to comments and using the pencil like a divining rod, pulling out of the blank sheet the image of what the words spoken by others might suggest. It is very important for facilitators to be exactly that: facilitators. At this stage of the charrette, proposing a solution is the worst thing for design facilitators to do, even if a solution appears obvious to them. Doing so now leaves the stakeholders behind and misses the value they bring to the process. I have seen charrettes short-circuited more often by overly aggressive design facilitators taking it upon themselves to "solve the problem" than by any other kind of facilitation failure. The bad feeling engendered among stakeholders when their role is not valued is almost impossible to repair after the fact. That is why the shift from talk phase to doodle phase cannot be rushed. The stakeholders must first trust the design facilitator to act as their agent, manifesting their hopes and dreams in physical form on the site. Absent time spent eliciting those hopes and dreams, no trust is possible.

Talking still dominates this stage, but it is done while drawing. Marking paper becomes ancillary to the conversation. In these circumstances, talking while drawing is as important as making eye contact while talking—and for some facilitators, it is just as natural. For most, however, combining right-brain (verbal) and left-brain (visual) activity at the same moment is notoriously difficult. But facilitators must find a way to talk and draw at the same time, even if it results in an embarrassingly halting conversation and a less than elegant diagram.

During this stage, facilitators must constantly refer to the design brief. If the brief contains a density target, the building form under discussion must be vetted for its capacity to meet that target. Design facilitators can delegate this "fact checker" role to a stakeholder and ask that person to ride herd on the group, ensuring that the group is on track to meet the targets. Participants with an analytical bent are often glad to play this role.

"Designer-Only" Time

During the second and subsequent days of the charrette, we often schedule "designer-only" times, typically toward the end of the day. One model has the full charrette team working from nine to five, with the facilitators continuing work after dinner. More often we allow the stakeholders to leave after lunch—say, at 2 P.M.—on the second and third days. The facilitators explain that this allows them to "clean up the drawings" in preparation for the next day's work. That is true, but it also allows the facilitators to make good progress without having to work directly with stakeholders the whole time. The facilitators can check in with one another during a brief meeting, discuss any personality issues that have emerged, speculate about what issues might be the most difficult to resolve, and share strategies for managing conflict. Designers can share quick and effective graphic techniques during these sessions. Designer-only sessions help facilitators align their styles and the content of their drawings so that charrette products, mostly drawings, are more uniform. Designers who work in professional offices often work in teams and learn to align products quickly to create a unified and comprehensive product; these sessions create times during the charrette for this to occur. The first designer-only session is a good time to discuss ways to use diagrams to resolve debates between stakeholders who hold different opinions on various site-related issues. In later sessions designers can report on how many of the required products are finished and which products might be difficult to complete in the time allowed, and for organizers to redistribute staff members and volunteer students (if available) to keep production on track. University design faculty and their students are less familiar with these absolute limits, so they tend to have more trouble operating within fixed time constraints.

The design facilitators also need a certain amount of time independent of the stakeholders to produce a drawn record of their investigations and conclusions, even at the earlier stage of the charrette. Initial conclusions shown in the form of green systems diagrams, for example, need to be captured and added to the body of information that supports the logic of the consensus plan. For facilitators who have not yet mastered the trick of talking and drawing at the same time, this designer-only time can be crucial.

The Third Design Stage: Doodle to Draw

By now, stakeholders and facilitators have most often become a working team. Occasionally there will still be personality conflicts to manage. We use simple techniques to overcome them: respectful side conversations, reshuffling of subteam composition, and providing those who lack team skills with specific tasks that allow them to work independently. However, the majority of stakeholder participants are likely to be more relaxed and cooperative as the outline of a consensus plan begins to emerge. Charrette participants incline toward consensus solutions at this stage without a specific acknowledgment of whose ideas are prevailing. Certainly some individuals are more effective than others in imagining and ultimately implementing a desirable outcome, but the important thing is that the charrette structure allows these visions to emerge without identifying a particular author, from the unspoken agreement of the whole.

In this prototypical charrette, by late in day two or early in day three, the doodles and diagrams provide a sound basis for more concrete proposals. Finally, the largely blank base map can be marked with the first lines of what will become the final proposal. Stream riparian setbacks can be drawn to flesh out the green infrastructure backbone. The basic lines of the interconnected street grid can be shown. Key urban locations can be more carefully designed, now informed by a consensus understanding of the appropriate housing mix, parking requirements, block size, and diversity of desired land uses. Breakout teams can work on these subtasks, with designated stakeholders or facilitators providing a liaison between groups to ensure compatibility among their designs. Check-in sessions after every four or five hours will help ensure that the design stays on track and that all members share a common sense of the emerging plan.

Eventually doodling gives way to drawing, and group conversation gives way to focused group production. At this point, facilitators should refer to the list of required products in the design brief. Stakeholders, facilitators, and any subteams should reflect on how they might complete those products. If the remaining time seems too short to complete the products listed, then facilitators and stakeholders should make a collective assessment of how close they can come and which products are most vital. This clearheaded conversation places the group "in the tunnel." That expression means that the participants are hurtling forward and will emerge on the other side at the deadline no matter what they do. They have only a certain amount of time and energy left; they must marshal and expend it strategically. At this stage, stakeholders and facilitators become extremely productive. Expert facilitation is required to identify gaps and inconsistencies in the group output and to encourage participants to fill in these gaps in time for the final presentation. There is no next day or next week to which to defer them.

Unfortunately, and inevitably, one or more of the participants will misinterpret the culture of the charrette and miss the shift from the talk phase to the draw phase. These people become more talkative instead of less as the deadline approaches. They wander from one table to another, peering over shoulders and initiating distracting conversations. Of all the many irritants facilitators can expect, for me this is the worst—worse by far than uncooperative, arrogant, and argumentative participants. Iconoclasts can be directed to make productive contributions; kibitzers cannot. Facilitators are well advised to be watchful for these types and try to direct their energies to some writing task early in the process.

The Midcourse Correction

We usually hold a "midcourse correction" about halfway through this type of charrette, usually at the end of day two or at the beginning of day three. We invite all of the participants in the pre-charrette workshops (the outer table), private sector leaders, and certain public officials to this meeting. The meeting is a very informal "pinup review," a chance to hold up preliminary ideas for review before it's too late to change them. The venue is usually the same room that is used for the charrette, with the larger group invited into the apparent chaos. No attempt at cleaning up the room is made, nor is one appropriate. Nevertheless, the content of the preliminary deliberations must be clearly communicated, as comments must be informed to be intelligent. Fortunately, the principles, goal, objectives, numerical requirements, and performance targets provide the logical armature for the presentation. Most of the guests will have participated in the creation of this framework, and they will recognize that the rough preliminary designs are emerging manifestations of the principles, goal, objectives, requirements, and targets in action. The preliminary ideas can be described, for example, as "in conformance with principle four in the following way," or "meeting the transportation objective by this means." If the numbers merit it, the informal presentation can be followed by breakout tables organized in the same groups as in the pre-charrette workshops. These individuals, by now quite comfortable in their familiar groups, can be asked to make suggestions and ultimately authorize the continuation of the charrette.

The basic question facilitators should ask at these tables is this: "Do you feel comfortable enough with the progress made by the team to support its moving forward?" The wording of the question is important. If the question is, "Do you love everything you see?" the answer will be no. But people are smart enough to know that they won't get everything they want. (If they weren't, voter participation in U.S. presidential elections would be close to zero.) The question, as posed, exhibits respect for the innate human ability to discern effective synthesis of often competing objectives. The answer, in effect, is likely to be: "Sure, it's not perfect, but of all the possible resolutions of the many apparently competing demands, it's pretty darn good!"

The Fourth Design Stage: "Draw Like Your Pants Are on Fire" and Final Presentation
By the middle of day three in the four-day charrette described here, the group is fully into the draw phase. Producing the final drawings and building the final presentation are really the same thing. In the last twenty-four hours, it's all about production, and it's all about the final show. Decisions are being made at breakneck speed, not only about how far to push design ideas to completion, but also about how completely it will be possible to describe those ideas to the larger group of stakeholders, officials, and citizens at large who are invited to the final presentation.

Pre-Presentation Team Meeting
We hold an all-team meeting about twenty-four hours prior to deadline to discuss the final presentation. This meeting helps us clarify the final product requirements and identifies key individuals who will accept responsibility for producing portions of the final presentation. It also helps focus the participants on making final decisions. The

basic outline of the presentation can be reviewed at this meeting and volunteers solicited to present key sections. Examples of previous presentations can be shown to reassure stakeholders that the task is achievable. Time is precious, so this meeting should take a half hour and never exceed an hour.

Templates

We typically supply two templates to help organize the flow of information to the final presentation and later to the final report (for examples of these and other templates mentioned, see the Web links in the appendix). The first template provides participants with a list of questions to answer. The questions are always grounded in the design brief, with a direct connection made to the goal, objectives, numerical requirements, and performance targets embodied therein. For instance, if the design brief includes a requirement to keep all dwelling units within a 5-minute walk of commercial services and transit, the question template would ask, "How did your team ensure that all new dwelling units were within a 5-minute walking distance of commercial services and transit?"

The second template provided is for the PowerPoint-based final presentation. We strongly believe that the final presentation must be captured digitally, as opposed to simply "hung," for two reasons. First, it provides an immediate and easy way to distribute a record of the charrette. Second, it provides a clearer way to organize and describe the charrette results than simply hanging drawings on a wall. We are aware that other charrette organizers allow participants to work to deadline and then hang up the drawings for public review while the ink is still wet. However exciting this may seem, it virtually ensures that the presentation will be incoherent, and the results, therefore, are more likely to be ephemeral.

To make it as easy as possible for stakeholders to flow their work into a polished final presentation, we provide a set of formatted slides ahead of time. Participants add text and images to spaces provided in the preformatted and headlined slides, which are organized in accordance with the design principles, objectives, requirements, and targets of the design brief. Organizing the presentation in this way grounds the results in the language of the charrette while making it clear that the proposal demonstrates what the site would look like if those principles and objectives were realized on the ground. In short, the pictures demonstrate the ideas, and the ideas are the essential core of the charrette.

Production Team Assistance

Bottlenecks in production are disastrous. There is nothing more frustrating for participants than lining up for a computer, waiting more than a few minutes to get a

During the final hours of the charrette, discussion ends and pure production ensues. Organizers must do whatever is necessary to both anticipate what will be needed during this phase and to supply anything that they did not anticipate immediately.

photo taken or an image scanned, or encountering technical problems when moving images from a data stick. With the clock ticking closer and closer to deadline. a charrette can easily implode just from technical frustrations. To prevent this, we provide a team of students and staff, both to support image processing and to ensure a more than adequate number of computers for participants. The sections of the presentation assigned to selected stakeholders will all flow together smoothly (if the facilitators have done their homework!) just before the final presentation.

Final Presentation

We usually schedule the final presentation for 7 P.M. on the last day of the charrette. This time is convenient for citizens, ensuring the largest possible crowd. It is always advantageous to turn out a large audience for the final presentation. It increases the energy of the participants to know that a large crowd of their supporters or potential detractors will be on hand. We believe that an audience of 200–400 outside observers, shored up with members of the outer table, provides the critical mass necessary to elevate the importance and impact of the charrette. Notices in the media will get the word out; direct mailing and, increasingly, the use of issue-focused e-mail lists are even more useful. Planning, design, and engineering consultants are likely to be very interested and can be contacted through their professional associations. City planning departments usually have long lists of committed and influential citizens who can and should be invited.

A large theater is required for this many people. High school auditoriums are often the best choice. They usually have advanced audiovisual equipment and more than 400 seats. As at all other events, refreshments must be provided—coffee, tea, and water at the very least.

It is usually a mistake for organizers or facilitators to do more than start off the presentation or wrap it up at the end, even though stakeholders often suggest that they take a more substantive role. This is an important time for the stakeholder participants to take ownership of the proposal in front of their peers in the community. Even if the presentations are flawed, it is far better hear your neighbor stumble through a heartfelt description of a possible shared future than to hear yet another dulcet-voiced outside expert telling you what's best for your town.

The final presentation should be no more than 2.5 hours long—ever. We try to confine the presentation of the proposal itself to an absolute maximum of 60 minutes. The presentation can be started off with the politically necessary "thank yous to the uninvolved," followed by short comments by the mayor or senior elected official of the municipality or district. Next is the presentation of the charrette proposal itself, broken up by geographic zones, issue areas, or charrette principles, with at least three different stakeholder presenters taking the stage. The presentation is immediately followed by a discussion featuring a respondents' panel made up of local luminaries and respected citizens. We ask the panel to answer previously provided questions; a typical example might be, "Do you think the results shown can be practically implemented, and, if so, what do you think stands in the way of their implementation right now?" The respondents' panel helps kick off a productive question and answer period and prevents the evening from being compromised if the first questioners have their own particular axe to grind (readers with a lot of experience at public meetings know that open microphones are a magnet for such individuals). Fifty minutes might be divided between the panel and the open-floor question and answer period. Just before bringing the session to a close, the organizers should tell the attendees what the next steps will be. At the very end, the mayor or some other luminary might close the session.

The final presentation should be held on a weekday evening. It should be well advertised, and refreshments should be provided, in the hope that it will be very well attended.

Afterparty

Although it's often late at night by this time, we always have an afterparty for the inner table and informally invited guests. This should be a party of the beer and pizza variety at a local pub. Design charrettes are intense experiences, and participants need a release after the final presentation. A pub is just the right venue. Not everyone feels compelled to go to such a seemingly impromptu event, so those who need to get home to their families are free to do so. In addition, when the party slowly evaporates, a pub is usually still filled with other revelers. Thus the party never feels dead, even if there are only two people from the charrette left. Obviously, cab rides are in order for those who stay the longest, or a designated volunteer might be enlisted to drive stalwart party animals home.

At the party, participants also get a chance to commit informally to follow-up action. It's only at this point that certain stakeholders will be fully convinced that their vision can be realized, and never before or after will they be charged up enough to plan their next moves so enthusiastically. A party at a pub is a far better way to capitalize on these possibilities than a boring and probably ill-attended follow-up meeting.

Variations on the Theme

For the sake of convenience and clarity, I have described the choreography of this prototypical charrette as if it were the only version possible. But in reality, we alter this basic framework almost every time. The flow of events stays generally the same. What changes is the exact makeup and duration of all the pieces and parts.

Designer-Only Time

Some of our implementation charrettes have "designer-only" times as described above. Others do not. The decision to do it one way or the other is based on many factors: Can you get stakeholders to stay all day? Are the stakeholders the type that cannot work effectively on the drawing parts of the process, so that it is better to have facilitators do all the drawings? Will having designer-only time reduce the esprit de corps of the team? Are the issues such that most of the charrette should be devoted to active negotiation among stakeholders in the room? The answers to all of these questions will have an influence on this decision.

Is It a Visioning Charrette?

The prototypical charrette described above is an implementation charrette. The choreography of a visioning charrette will differ in the following ways:

- The design brief will be reviewed by an advisory committee, rather than in pre-charrette workshops attended by stakeholders.
- The teams will be largely composed of designers and students rather than stakeholders.
- Drawn output should take priority over negotiations, as drawings are the sine qua non of visioning charrettes.
- The final presentation is of great importance and should be widely advertised, as this is the best chance to involve the community in the process.
- It is understood that the charrette proposal is an educational, as opposed to a regulatory, tool.

Charrette Duration

The prototypical charrette described above takes place over four days split by a weekend. This is our most common model, but there are others:

- Four continuous days
- Three continuous days

- Five continuous days, with the weekend set aside for designers to assemble information for a Monday presentation

The choice of one or the other of these formats is influenced by many factors: the budget, the availability and commitment of stakeholders, the complexity of the problem, and the final product requirements being the most important of these.

Clearly, then, there are many possible combinations of charrette components, but all of the variations share the same list of process imperatives: enough time must be allowed to transform stakeholders into team members; the progress from talk to doodle to draw must not be rushed; design facilitators must be there to make manifest a collective vision, not to impose their own will; technical frustrations must be eliminated; a firm grounding in policy and the work of the preliminary workshops allows the charrette proposal to "design itself"; ways must be found to include a larger circle of people in the charrette than the fifteen or twenty that can gather around a table; and finally, presentations are formal events that should be treated with the respect appropriate to their potential impact.

7. After the Charrette

A charrette is only as good as what happens after it's over. All too often charrettes conclude with no clear plans as to how to transform the design ideas generated into the policies necessary to implement them. Even visioning charrettes deserve a clear strategy for dissemination if any features of the vision generated are to be realized. Thus the plan for the charrette should include post-charrette activities. For implementation charrettes, additional "mini-charrette" sessions with the design team and relevant officials might be required to work through difficult issues left unresolved at the main charrette. Targeted research may be necessary to answer crucial questions. Ideally, the design team will reconvene with implementation agents (developers, staff engineers, traffic planners, environmental regulators, planning board members) a number of times after the charrette. As the project moves toward implementation, there is a natural tendency for innovations to be watered down as more conservative impulses take hold. Officially sanctioned charrette follow-up sessions let stakeholders explain to a different audience the rationale for the plan and how it affects specific technical issues.

Preliminary Charrette Report

The organizers should deliver a preliminary charrette report to the project sponsors within a week to ten days after the final presentation. Wait too long, and the report becomes disconnected from the public attention the project has garnered; stakeholders can be left feeling that nothing resulted from their efforts in such a case. Preliminary reports from our charrettes are provided in the appendix. Some of these are titled final charrette report when in fact they are preliminary and are followed later by a more substantial piece of work often worthy of inclusion into a city's regulatory tools. For the purpose of this book all products that are delivered immediately after the charrette are preliminary, to distinguish them from the more elaborate, detailed, and extensively reviewed final reports listed separately.

A charrette is in some ways equivalent to a political campaign: chances for victory in a political campaign and chances for the implementation of charrette results are both enhanced if you control the message and keep the message in front of the public. The message of the charrette is the design proposal itself and the principles, goal, and objectives on which it is based. The easiest and most appropriate way to get this message out is to reuse the final presentation PowerPoint as the framework for the preliminary report. A typical report would consist of 25–40 pages based on the charrette presentation and following its exact format, starting with principles, then describing goal, objectives, numerical requirements, and performance targets. A horizontal, or landscape format, report (long axis of the page sideways) is the easiest style of report to produce, as this format presumably correlates with the final presentation slides, which would therefore be easy to adapt for this purpose. The preliminary report can and should be easy to digest, with clear, "headline-able" conclusions highlighted in the text.

Assuming the project sponsors have no objections, this report can and should be distributed widely. Newspaper reporters who were too busy to cover the final presentation can write from this report; efficiency is paramount for them. Members of the charrette inner table and the broader audience of stakeholders who participated in other events should also receive the report, as should elected and appointed officials who were exposed to the process. Finally, this report and all others produced by the project should be placed on a project Web site. We build a separate Web site for each charrette we conduct, largely to allow interested people an easy way to access all the products generated. Links to a number of these charrette Web sites can be found in the appendix.

City councils and other legislative and jurisdictional bodies may never be more interested in knowing the results of the charrette than immediately after its completion. Using the report as a "leave-behind" is an important way to ensure that council members have this information in an easy-to-digest format—one that they can understand, retain, and explain to others if called upon. In the best of circumstances, the report can be the basis for council action. A council motion to forward the findings to the city planning department for action would be one felicitous outcome.

Final Plan

Once this preliminary report is completed and distributed, organizers can turn their attention to the final plan. There are two basic types of final plans: the final *concept plan*, which, as the name suggests, explicates the concepts generated at the charrette; and the *implementation plan*, which also explains the concepts generated at the charrette but in a way that can be used to regulate development of the site. Different municipalities call these different types of plans different things according to their own local conventions, which may be confusing to charrette organizers. Host municipalities will certainly have their own nomenclature and experience in these two report forms, so they can help. Despite the differences in nomenclature, we can describe certain features that distinguish the two types of plans. Both are intended for the same audience of decision makers and stakeholders and are thus relatively specialized in content and tone; yet we try to make them understandable to an interested lay audience, both to increase their impact and to increase the number of supporters who might make reference to the plan.

Concept Plan

We define a concept plan as one that describes the charrette proposal, but in a narrative and didactic form. It is designed to teach and inform rather than to regulate. We often organize a final concept plan in conformance with the structure of the design brief—that is, around the issues of transportation, green infrastructure, building and land use, sense of place, and energy—or around the principles, goal, objectives, numerical requirements, and performance targets of the brief. Concept plans are always produced in close association with municipal officials to insure alignment with their regulatory environment. Table 7.1 shows a typical and informative table of contents from the final concept plan produced by our Squamish Smart Growth on the Ground design charrette.

The bulk of the Squamish Smart Growth on the Ground charrette effort is described in section 4 of the above-referenced plan, under the headings "Moving Around," "Allocating Land Uses," and "Place Making." In this case, the ecological and energy issues are threaded through the subsections rather than commanding discrete sections. (The full concept plan is accessible via the link to the project Web site in the appendix.)

The concept plan provides a good opportunity to describe process issues and to publish targeted research in an enduring form. The tone of the text is narrative, didactic,

Table 7.1

Downtown Squamish Concept Plan

Table of Contents

Four Page Summary (distributed in January 13, 2006 edition of *Squamish Chief*)

Section 1. The Big Picture—Executive Summary

Section 2. Introducing the Project

Section 3. Making the Concept Plan

Section 4. The Concept Plan

4.1	Framework
4.2	Moving Around
4.2.1	District Road Network
4.2.2	Downtown Road Network
4.2.3	Transit
4.2.4	Trail Network
4.2.5	Crossings
4.3	Allocating Land Uses
4.4	Place Making

Section 5. Taking the Next Steps

Appendices

    Appendix 1. Design Brief

    Appendix 2. Supporting Technical Documents for Targets

    Appendix 3. Sustainability Indicators Base Case Scenario

    Appendix 4. Foundation Research Bulletins

    Appendix 5. Development Opportunities in Downtown Squamish

    Appendix 6. Eco-Industrial Networking in Squamish

    Appendix 7. Charrette Team

and qualitative, as opposed to the imperative, prescriptive, and empirical tone of an implementation plan (discussed below). Organizers and project sponsors must be clear on the purpose of the concept plan. If it is to educate and explain, it should be written in qualitative, lucid, and explicatory tones, creating an educational narrative that explains the charrette and leaves the reader convinced of the merit of the design. If it is to regulate, it should be quantitative, precise, technical, and defensible.

Table 7.2
East Clayton Neighbourhood Concept Plan (NCP)
CONTENTS
1.0 INTRODUCTION
      1.1 Purpose of Report
      1.2 The Planning Context
      1.3 The Clayton General Land Use Plan
      1.4 The East Clayton Integrated Planning Process
      1.5 Process Objectives
      1.6 Supplementary Follow-up Projects

2.0 BACKGROUND
      2.1 Historic Settlement Pattern of Surrey
      2.2 Cultural History of Clayton
      2.3 Site Location/Context
      2.4 Existing Land Uses
      2.5 Topography
      2.6 Vegetation
      2.7 Soils
      2.8 Streams and Hydrology

3.0 DESCRIPTION OF THE EAST CLAYTON LAND USE PLAN
      3.1 Sustainable Planning Principles
      3.2 Land Use Types

4.0 LAND USE AND DEVELOPMENT PERFORMANCE
STANDARDS AND DESIGN GUIDELINES
      4.1 Residential Areas
      4.2 Commercial Areas
      4.3 Live/Work—Work/Live Areas
      4.4 Techno-Business Park Area

5.0 ECOLOGICAL INFRASTRUCTURE PERFORMANCE
STANDARDS AND GUIDELINES
      5.1 Building Sites—Performance Objectives

8.0 COMMUNITY SERVICES AND AMENITIES
    8.1 General
    8.2 Parkland Development
    8.3 Library and Library Materials
    8.4 Fire and Police Protection
    8.5 Summary of Funding Arrangements

9.0
    9.6 City Project Team
    9.7 Design Guidelines—Neighbourhood Character Studies and
        Registered Building Schemes
    9.8 Live/Work and Work/Live Developments
    9.9 Coach Houses and Other Ancillary Dwelling Units
        East Clayton NCP
        Engineering Servicing Plan Report
    9.10 Community Infrastructure Maintenance Plan and
        Community Stewardship

Implementation Plan

We define an implementation plan as one that describes the charrette proposal, but in instrumental and regulatory terms. It is designed to clearly regulate rather than inform or educate. We format implementation plans according to templates already in use by the host municipality, respecting the culture of regulation already in place. To this format we add the minimum sections necessary to ensure that the broader objectives of the sustainable community design charrette are met. Table 7.2 shows a typical and informative table of contents from the (inappropriately named)[1] East Clayton Neighbourhood Concept Plan (NCP), produced for the City of Surrey, British Columbia.

It should be immediately apparent that the implementation plan is a much more extensive, technical, and complex document than the concept plan. It takes more time to produce, and as a result, it is more expensive. But this is no surprise. Expensive plans for new development or redeveloped areas are the norm. Overall, design charrettes provide significant savings in time and money when compared with conventional planning processes. The charrette radically accelerates the public review process and eliminates the need for the full professional development of alternative schemes as well as the expensive preparation of those schemes for often rancorous public hearings. Thus, while seemingly expensive, it is cheaper than the status quo alternative.

Our implementation plans exceed the requirements set for preplanning new greenfield or redevelopment areas. Municipalities typically ask for a detailed assessment of the sewer, water, road, and drainage infrastructure required before allowing development to proceed. Any implementation plan generated in a charrette must incorporate these features. In many jurisdictions, this expensive engineering work is paid for not by the municipality, but by the proponent as part of the approval process.

In Surrey, engineering information of the kind contained in the East Clayton NCP is typically submitted by consulting engineers under contract with the city (a local engineering firm that is paid from permitting fees charged to development proponents). As planning departments have become more and more sophisticated, particularly in municipalities like Surrey that are experiencing rapid growth, they have expanded the scope of these documents beyond the traditional engineering imperatives of sewer, water, road, and drainage infrastructure to include detailed land use and open space plans. They now frequently concern themselves with additional issues such as parks, natural area protection, special land use controls (as on home offices), and design guidelines for buildings and landscaping. Implementation plans such as the East Clayton NCP take these concerns a big step further, describing a collaboratively generated synthetic community design plan based on sustainability principles.

Sections 6, 7, and 8 of the East Clayton NCP constitute the more traditional sections of the plan and were written by the city's engineering consultants. These consultants were crucial members of the charrette team and participated in the entire charrette process (the city agreed to pay their fees for the time they spent attending the workshops and the charrette and performing the detailed work contained in these sections of the plan).

The engineering work contained in sections 6, 7, and 8 provided precise and professionally defensible answers to traditional infrastructure questions, but was unique in that it incorporated a number of the more provocative and innovative strategies emerging from the charrette. These strategies included narrow streets in an interconnected street grid, rear lanes, and natural storm drain systems. These innovations were untested in regional jurisdictions, so they naturally engendered anxiety for city staff and consultant engineers, because these people are held accountable for the regulations contained in plans such as these. Any changes in standards, however minor they seem, are likely to provoke a cautionary response. As mentioned before, this anxiety constitutes a major—perhaps *the* major—impediment to change. Organizers must be realistic, but also committed to making change happen. They must not lose heart when this anxiety emerges—and it will. Close collaboration between charrette organizers, city staff, and consultant engineers is the ideal way to ensure that the holistic thinking embodied in the charrette plan is not undercut during this more technical, risk-averse, and conservative phase of the process.

The East Clayton NCP added to or substantially expanded the categories included in the usual neighborhood concept plan, including green infrastructure performance targets, environmental protection, mixed-use development, live/work housing, and urban design codes governing the form and design of structures. A careful review of the language used in these sections provides a useful guide for others. The entire plan is accessible via a Web link in the appendix.

In summary, there are several crucial differences between the East Clayton NCP and previous planning control documents in Surrey and elsewhere in North America: While typical regulations describe how land use activities are to be separated, this plan describes how they are to be combined. While typical transportation plans assume that road and movement systems should be hierarchical, unimodal, and dendritic, this plan assumes that interconnection and multiple modes of transportation are the goal. While typical parcel development plans assume that separation of buildings from one another and the public realm is desirable, this plan assumes that the opposite is true. While typical open space plans discuss the provision of open space as if parks were commodities to buy in certain predetermined packages and place randomly in the landscape, this plan provides an ecological framework for both protecting and capitalizing on the green infrastructure of the site. Finally, while most plans are silent on issues of building form and the relationship of buildings to street, parcel, and block, this plan provides defensible requirements that, when followed, will ensure that the aesthetic, social, and safety objectives of the plan are achieved.

The East Clayton NCP diverged so markedly from conventional plans with respect to mixed land uses, road network design, and green infrastructure that it took two years to pass through the Surrey City Council. During that time, and entirely because of the deliberations associated with the plan, Surrey passed bylaw changes that applied not just to East Clayton, but to the whole city, including blanket legalization of freehold townhouse and secondary suites (rental units contained within single-family homes).

This example shows not only how effectively the charrette process can catalyze wider change, but also how deeply embedded are the structures that resist it. We advise organizers to anticipate this resistance when planning charrettes and to assume that an implementation plan will be a necessary precondition for implementation, and therefore for success. Organizers must not be dismayed at the inherently conservative discourse they will encounter during this stage. Change is dangerous for city staff and consultant engineers—they know from experience that they can lose jobs, get sued, and harm their families if they deviate from status quo norms. Empathy for their position is a crucial precondition for facilitators who want to work within this highly conservative milieu.

The budgets associated with delivering an implementation plan can seem daunting, but as we pointed out earlier, municipalities and developers typically spend hundreds of thousands of dollars producing infrastructure plans for new developments. These expenditures usually produce cookie-cutter plans for one sprawling and unsustainable district after another. For the same amount of time and money, we can help turn this ponderous ship around and steer it toward measurably more sustainable results.

Mini-Charrettes

The prototypical charrette described in chapter 6 almost always ends in consensus. This consensus incorporates a good-faith understanding among charrette participants that the plan and its components are workable and that the details of those components can be resolved by staff and their consultants in later weeks and months. These details are left as "issues outstanding." Unfortunately, later work on these usually technical outstanding issues almost always elicits the most conservative impulses in city staff and their consulting engineers. Thus it is probable that when they revisit these issues after the charrette, their responses will be more cautious. Remember that integration and synthesis is the essence of the charrette and is embedded in the details of the design, right down to street edge details. This integrity can be easily compromised by seemingly minor changes. We recommend reconvening the charrette team in a mini-charrette to prevent that integrity from dying the death of a thousand cuts.

Mini-charrettes should be about a half day in duration and bring together all of the charrette participants and any new consultants who now have a role in the project. Technical issues should be unpacked carefully in the presence of city staff and consultants, with all of their anxieties and concerns laid out in great detail. Senior management staff should be involved at the highest level possible. Elected officials may be involved if they were involved in the charrette. High-level involvement is necessary to ensure that those individuals with the broadest scope of understanding and responsibility weigh in. Senior managers in the planning and engineering departments, and elected officials generally, have more ability and opportunity than middle-level staff or consultants to think laterally and broadly about community development issues. Additionally, with senior officials involved in the deliberations, the weight of decisions is at least partially removed from the shoulders of middle-level staff and consultants. This freedom from sole responsibility reduces the often stultifying influence of risk avoidance on decisions. With shared responsibility, the risk is more fairly distributed.

Depending on the issue, the table of the whole at the mini-charrette might be divided into two or more breakout tables for subtasks. Even seemingly minor issues such as the design for an infiltration storm drain system are remarkably complex when unpacked and lend themselves to detailed examination of the component elements. As always, the division into breakout tables must be followed by a generous "reporting session" to ensure that synthesis is not compromised by excessive silo thinking.

Agreement is the product of the mini-charrette. That agreement can be in the form of words or diagrams or both. A clear record of the agreement in the form of a short report, memorandum of understanding, or official minutes should be part of the service provided by the organizers. It is very important to provide for this service in the scope of services contract and the associated memorandum of understanding between the organizers and the charrette sponsors.

Strategic Targeted Research

Technical bulletins should be incorporated into the design brief development phase, as discussed in chapter 4. However, certain "issues outstanding" generate a need for post-charrette research and bulletin production. Often this need is tied to the same outstanding issues that precipitate a need for mini-charrettes. In such instances, charrette organizers can produce one or more technical bulletins written in language that all stakeholders can understand. Our technical bulletin comparing front driveway and rear lane access (accessible via a Web link in the appendix) is an example.

Producing technical bulletins can be time-consuming; our technical bulletin on rear lane access took over a week of staff time to produce. Unfortunately, there were no similar comparisons to be found in the literature, and careful drawings and area computations were required. This time expenditure should be allowed for when developing the scope of services contract for the project, but that is easier said than done. At the beginning of the process, organizers have no idea which issues will be outstanding and whether one or more issues will require strategic targeted research. An open-ended provision for a "fee for additional services" as required would solve the problem if host communities were open to it. In practice, few are. Consequently, we often provide this service without any additional fee, assigning the hours to overhead and acknowledging that the research has a value for future projects or for dissemination to the field. This approach is particularly fitting within academic research units like ours. We have an overarching mandate to disseminate our findings broadly with little regard for intellectual property rights. Producing these research findings and, indeed, advancing the quality and efficacy of our contribution to solving the problems of our times is central to our mission.

Conclusion

Sustainable communities cannot be designed using the same methods that produced unsustainable ones. Whatever method we use must be inclusive, synthetic, and capable of tolerating the unavoidable ambiguities that are the defining quality of any complex system. Inhabited landscapes—cities, in other words—are among the most complex systems imaginable. The charrette method described herein is inclusive, synthetic, and accepts ambiguity. It operates not on proofs, but on consensus, and it depends on holistic thinking first and linear methodologies second. It moves in the right direction, from the whole of the city to the parts necessary to build it, not the other way around.

Charrettes are a key manifestation of what must be a broadly based paradigm shift in the way we build cities. Charrettes and other collaborative and integrative methods must no longer be exceptional events held rarely, if ever; instead, they must become the new way of planning cities. Without a substantial and broadly based paradigm shift in the planning field, there is little hope we can plan the sustainable cities our children need, and which will be necessary to help cool a rapidly overheating planet. We hope that this book has in some small way contributed to this paradigm shift and this more hopeful future.

Location: East Clayton is located in the City of Surrey, British Columbia, at Fraser Highway and 188th Street.

Project duration from first workshop to completed charrette: January 15–May 11, 1999.

Duration of charrette event: May 6–11, exclusive of May 8 and 9 (four-day charrette).

Charrette type: Implementation charrette to produce governing Neighbourhood Concept Plan (NCP).

Facilitation: Design Centre for Sustainability, University of British Columbia, for design facilitation and project choreography; Pacific Resources, Inc., for public process facilitation, communication, conflict resolution, and outreach.

Charrette format:
The East Clayton charrette was an implementation charrette. There was one large team with all members working toward the goal of consensus on one implementable design.

Site:
The site consisted of 620 acres of upland "acreage" lots of 1–20 acres. Formerly farmland, the area is now uncultivated land owned by over 80 separate landowners. The land lies within the Surrey corporate boundary but

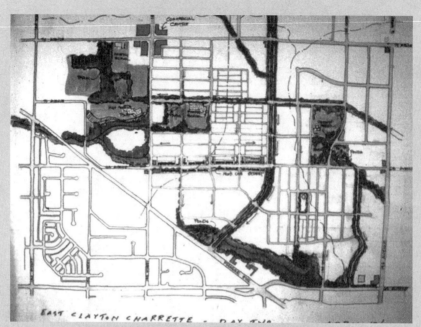

First consensus drawing from the East Clayton Sustainable Community Design Charrette. The beauty of this drawing lies not in its graphic elegance, but in the process and consensus it represents. Dashed lines represent separate watersheds that were critical to understanding the site's ecological function. Alternative block diagrams (shown on page 133) represent the lengthy struggle of the charrette team to understand the forgotten logic of the grid and rear lane street pattern. Large green blocks represent the key pieces of green infrastructure appropriate to each watershed.

is unserviced (has no infrastructure for providing city water and sewer services). The area was one of fifteen separate areas in the city about to be brought into the service district.

Client:

The City of Surrey engaged the UBC Design Centre and Pacific Resources to partner with it in the context of its usual Neighbourhood Concept Planning process.

Client goal:

The City of Surrey's planning department was looking for a way to integrate more sustainable practices into its usual processes for authorizing and regulating development of unserviced areas. The UBC Design Centre for Sustainability had been working in Surrey and building trust for three years, first through the Sustainable Urban Landscapes, Surrey Design Charrette and later through the Alternative Development Standards workshop (Web links to both projects are given in the appendix). The seven principles for sustainability that came out of that work were ultimately adopted by the Surrey City Council to guide the East Clayton initiative. UBC selected Surrey from a host of other municipal applicants who also wanted to develop more sustainable communities. UBC came with its own funding, so there was no charge for our services to the community. The East Clayton area was subject to development restriction if the ecological performance of the new community's storm system could not dramatically exceed conventional performance. Downstream soil saturation in agricultural floodplain lands, caused by upland urbanization, had become severe. The green infrastructure strategies embodied in principles 6 and 7 below offered a possible way of resolving this problem.

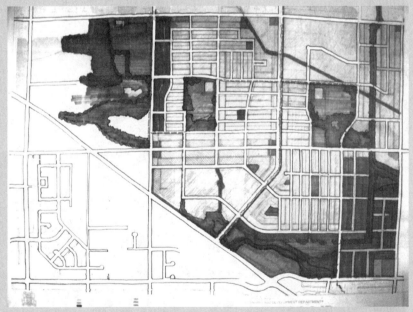

Day four plan from the East Clayton charrette. The interconnected street grid and green infrastructure system have been resolved. Land uses are close to their final resolution. This more traditional drawing is close to regulatory instrument quality.

Participants:

Forty stakeholders from various communities of interest participated, including developers, City of Surrey planning and engineering officials, City of Surrey operations staff, environmental regulators, school district officials, and representatives of higher levels of government.

Political context:

Individuals at various levels of government and within the citizenry of British Columbia had become frustrated with the lack of progress in achieving their higher-level goals on the ground. Various provincial initiatives had produced a robust body of policy supporting sustainable community development principles. The challenge remained applying those principles to site-scale projects. The UBC Design Centre had been promoting the application of those principles on the ground for a number of years. Design Centre advisory board members from various levels of government encouraged the Design Centre to take up the challenge of getting a sustainable community built. Sufficient grant money for the charrette was secured from foundations and multiple branches of government. Meanwhile, the City of Surrey had been struggling on its own to understand what sustainability meant "on the ground." The work of the Design Centre offered a low-risk to no-risk way (i.e., no cost and an ability to opt out at any time) to experiment with implementing sustainability principles. The Surrey City Council, at the behest of city staff, authorized a sustainable community design initiative and formally requested a planning partnership with UBC at that time.

Project principles:

The following principles existed prior to the East Clayton charrette. They were the product of a series of prior events, most significantly the Sustainable Urban Landscapes, Surrey Design Charrette:

1. Increase density to conserve energy by the design of compact walkable neighbourhoods to encourage pedestrian activities where basic services (schools, parks, transit, shops, etc.) are within 5 to 6 minutes walking distance from their homes.

The final regulatory plan produced by City of Surrey staff after the East Clayton charrette. This plan is now being used to guide rezoning for the site. Only tiny changes were made from the consensus plan.

2. Different dwelling types (a mix of housing types, a broad range of densities from single-family homes to apartment buildings) in the same neighbourhood and even on the same street.

3. Communities designed for people; therefore all dwellings present a friendly face to the street to promote social interaction.

4. Car storage and services handled in lanes at the rear of dwellings.

5. Interconnected street network, in a grid or modified grid pattern, to provide for a variety of itineraries and to disperse traffic congestion; and public transit to connect with the surrounding region.

6. Narrow streets shaded by rows of trees to save costs and to provide a greener and friendlier environment.

7. Preservation of the natural environment and promotion of natural drainage systems where stormwater is held on the surface and permitted to seep naturally into the ground.

The Surrey City Council reviewed these principles and unanimously approved them as the basis for the new initiative. It is worth noting that in one way or another, various city standards, regulations, and bylaws conspired to make achieving all of these principles either impossible or illegal prior to the charrette. The council, in effect, had voted against almost the entire body of regulations it oversaw.

Project goal:

To build a community in the East Clayton area of Surrey that meets local, provincial, and federal policy objectives for sustainable development.

This goal statement is ideal: short and to the point. It clearly makes the point that we have good policies for sustainability, but nothing on the ground that demonstrates them.

Project objectives:

1. Produce a more sustainable community design model for Surrey and other British Columbia communities.

2. Work out and resolve the contradictions between often contradictory sustainability policy objectives.

East Clayton
Neighbourhood Concept Plan

50   0   50 100   200 meters

Nov. 1999

Illustrative site plan produced for the East Clayton Neighborhood Concept Plan after the charrette. Although it is very time-consuming, we always try to determine the exact building footprints for all new buildings, in the belief that absent this, you have no way of knowing, or communicating, what the community will look like.

3. Demonstrate the connection between sustainability and desirability.
4. Resolve the conflicts between typical community subdivision and site and traffic engineering regulations and sustainability design objectives.
5. Create a setting where designers can facilitate resolutions between those agencies and entities whose mandates can often be in conflict.
6. Broadly disseminate the results of this process through a variety of means and venues—to citizens, elected representatives, policymakers, and designers— and thereby influence the future urban development of our region.

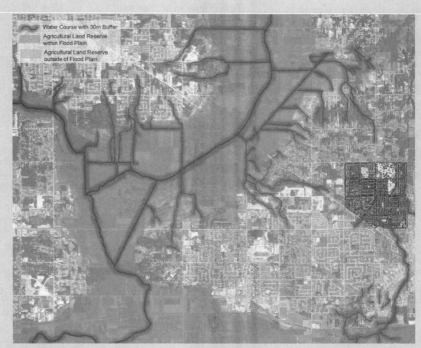

Water Course with 30m Buffer
Agricultural Land Reserve within Flood Plain
Agricultural Land Reserve outside of Flood Plain

The final design for East Clayton, shown situated in its larger ecological and cultural context. Its relationship to different watersheds and agricultural lowlands is apparent in this larger view.

These objectives also supply a good model. They speak to the issues necessary to meet the goal and what the value of meeting the goal might be. They are also few in number, which allows charrette participants to internalize them and use them for thinking about and speaking to the issues before them.

Summary of numerical requirements and performance targets:

Residential density:

Average gross density of 10 dwelling units per acre in a variety of house types (industrial zones and existing 1970s one-acre subdivision are not included in this calculation). House types range from a lowest density of 8 dwelling units per acre gross (for single-family homes) to a high of 45 dwelling units per acre (for four-story apartment buildings). Residential units were blended and mixed to promote integration into the fabric of the neighborhood. Over 5,000 housing units will eventually be built.

Jobs:

The jobs target for the city is one job per household. Progress is being made to reach this goal, making Surrey more of a center than a suburb. This same one job per household is also the jobs target used for the site. This explains why 40 acres are devoted to job sites and an additional 20 acres to live/work sites. Commercial areas in the district are also important generators of jobs.

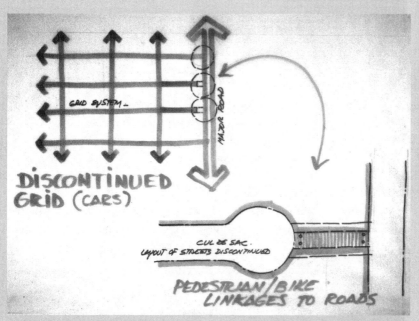

The most contentious issue at the East Clayton charrette was the relative merits of the block and lane versus the cul-de-sac street pattern. Many were concerned that grids and lanes would foster crime. A series of well-publicized attacks that had occurred recently, all in Vancouver lanes, exacerbated this view. These and other issues of this type will always arise at charrettes. Organizers must spend whatever time is necessary to resolve them. This diagram was produced by a charrette facilitator to capture the comments made by stakeholders in graphic form.

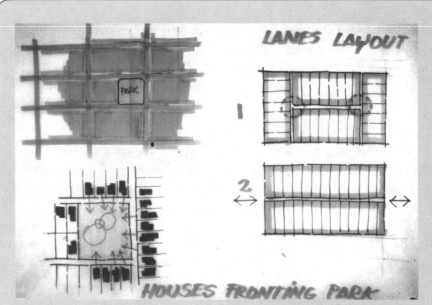

Perceived issues of safety led to the production of these diagrammatic explorations. Lanes with clear visual access all the way through were preferred (option 2) over T or H pattern lanes. Observation over small parks from front windows was built into the design. Interestingly, police personnel purchased housing in the first phase in great numbers. The defensible space concerns that were so compelling in the charrette were reflected in the design in a way that police seemed to instinctively recognize.

Transportation:

An interconnected street system is the crucial feature contributing to sustainable transportation. The East Clayton project breaks radically with the dendritic street network that characterizes the surrounding neighborhood. The block size is small, averaging 500 by 280 feet, maximizing route options and availability of on-street parking. Rear lanes are provided in most blocks to make streets safer for pedestrians and create a more socially interactive and safer streetscape. Once the district is populated and bus service expanded, all dwelling units will be no more than a 5-minute walk to transit services.

Environmental:

The site contains the headwaters for three different stream systems. All the receiving streams are salmon-bearing streams and sensitive to disruption. Downstream agricultural lands are subject to oversaturation from upland urban stormwater, requiring a change in conventional storm drain infrastructure standards. The solution for both the salmon problem and the agricultural flooding problem was the same: infiltrate the first inch of all rainwater that falls on the site. This strategy will capture and infiltrate 90 percent of all water that falls on the site and maintain the watershed hydrograph close to its predevelopment condition. The green infrastructure system incorporates streets, parks, and natural areas into an integrated system patterned on natural system function.

Charrette process/choreography:

Six workshops were held with separate communities of interest prior to the charrette. Their purpose was to review the project principles and the charrette design brief and suggest any changes necessary. The total number of stakeholders who participated in these workshops was over sixty. Community-of-interest tables ("the outer table") elected representatives to participate in the charrette ("the inner table"). Thirteen stakeholders participated in the charrette with four local professional design facilitators and three process facilitators. The charrette consumed five full days, with a midcourse correction at the end of the third day. The final presentation was held the following week before a large audience of stakeholders, citizens, and elected officials. Two additional public hearings were held in the following two months. Two "mini-charrettes" were organized to deal with two "issues outstanding": the presence of rear lanes and the details of the infiltration storm drain system.

Charrette products:

Consensus plan: The consensus plan constituted the single most important product of the charrette. Most of the attention at the charrette was focused on producing this one drawing.

Rough consensus street sections: A great deal of time also went into evaluating various alternative infiltration street sections. Infiltration streets were installed in East Clayton and have met the performance target of 1 inch per day infiltration. Their design was the result of this consensus. Follow-up illustrative plan to illustrate all parcels and probable building sites.

Approved Neighbourhood Concept Plan: The UBC Design Centre collaborated with the City of Surrey on the region's first regulatory instrument to promote a sustainable neighborhood: the East Clayton Neighbourhood Concept Plan. The plan was submitted to the city three months after the charrette. Staff amendments and council consideration required an additional two years before passage. The Neighbourhood Concept Plan is accessible via a Web link in the appendix.

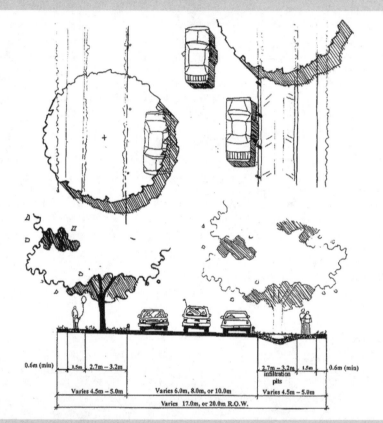

Curbless infiltration "green street" design approved at the charrette. This drawing shows a queuing street with parking on both sides and a 15-foot-wide two-way travel lane. The concept called for tipping the roadway to one side only ("cross pitch") to the infiltration swale shown on the right. The performance target was a 1 inch per day infiltration capacity. Subsurface treatment was not determined at the charrette, but rather left as an "issue outstanding," and is thus not shown.

Current status:

The final NCP was passed by the Surrey City Council in 2002. The first phase of building started in 2002. The entire project area is currently over 25 percent complete. All of the developers' concerns about marketing a sustainable neighborhood have been successfully overcome. The project is outcompeting its more conventional rivals on adjacent sites. Many of the innovations proposed and implemented here have been applied throughout the city. Bylaws and regulations to enable secondary suites and infiltration storm drainage systems throughout the city have been passed by the City Council. The project is seen as a highly successful model for more sustainable development. About half of all new single-family homes in East Clayton contain rental suites. On the downside, the mix of housing types has not been as diverse as desired, the commercial sites identified near the first phase have been slow to develop, and the infiltration storm drain system originally proposed at the charrette was changed after the charrette to a system that includes curbs and is therefore more expensive than the one originally designed.

A street in the first phase of construction in East Clayton. The 35 by 100 foot parcels with lanes in the rear leave the street front available for front porches and uninterrupted by dangerous cub cuts.

Certain streets attain income distribution and higher density through the provision of secondary suites on the parcel, in this case over the garage. This form is only possible if the minimum off-street parking requirements are reduced to a more reasonable one parking space per unit from the more typical two or three.

Lessons learned:
- Those who are currently responsible for sprawl—developers, regulators, and city officials—are willing to try a very different approach. In our experience, sprawl has few defenders among the people responsible for its creation.
- Although all agree there is a problem, there is strong difference of opinion about what to do about it, and what can and should be changed.
- A great deal of time is needed to talk through the detail issues of sustainable design. Things such as the presence or absence of curbs, or rear lanes, or the width of the average lot can become very complicated and contentious very fast. Linking these seemingly small decisions to the sustainability principles is the central challenge for facilitators of implementation charrettes. Details are tremendously important.
- It is important for charrette organizers to maintain a role for themselves and the charrette team after the charrette if at all possible. Absent this,

it is inevitable that more conventional responses will begin to erode the design advances made at the charrette, dragging the project back toward status quo standards. Mini-charrette follow-ups and required review by charrette participants before approval would help.

- Suburban sprawl can be changed, and multiparty integrated decision-making processes (such as charrettes) are the most effective catalyst for making it happen. Charrette methods would need to be institutionalized in every city for this to occur. This transformation is happening, but not fast enough. Ways are needed to accelerate this transformation.
- Foundation and higher-level government support is needed for this type of initiative, as municipalities rarely feel they have the "extra resources" for this kind of event, even though it is demonstrably more efficient than conventional models.
- Trust is your most valuable commodity. Outside design charrette facilitators must be trusted as fair and open, even if they do have an agenda (such as sustainability) to advance.

Location: The greater Damascus area is located approximately 12 miles (20 kilometers) southeast of downtown Portland, Oregon.

The Damascus Area Design Workshop site in the southeast corner of the Portland, Oregon, metropolitan area. The 15,000-acre site is now slated for urban expansion, with its population expected to increase from 12,000 to over 100,000 residents.

Project duration from first workshop to completed charrette: April 1–June 3, 2002.

Duration of charrette event: May 29–June 3 inclusive (six-day charrette) Charrette type: Visioning charrette with stakeholders in the majority to ensure that those who reviewed the materials later would appreciate the practicality of a vision generated not by designers, but rather by involved stakeholders. At the same time, there was never an intention that the exact design be implemented by regional authorities; rather, the intention was to influence their deliberations.

Facilitation: Three teams of designers, landscape architects, and architects were brought in for their special expertise. Half were from the Portland area; the other half were from other parts of North America.

Charrette format:
The Damascus Area Design Workshop was a visioning charrette. Three teams worked independently, with frequent reporting back to whole group, toward the goal of one final proposal.

Site:
The site consisted of approximately 6,000 hectares (15,000 acres) of farm fields, forests, and low-density residential development in a landscape interrupted by stream channels traversing the valleys and prominent butte formations. The Clackamas River forms the southern boarder of the site. The area is owned by over 200 separate landowners on lots typically larger than 1 acre.

Client:
1000 Friends of Oregon and the Coalition for a Livable Future. 1000 Friends of Oregon was established in the 1970s to protect gains made consequent to Senate Bill 100, the seminal Oregon land use law. The Coalition for a Livable Future is a coalition of nongovernmental organizations united to develop common strategies for solving regional problems.

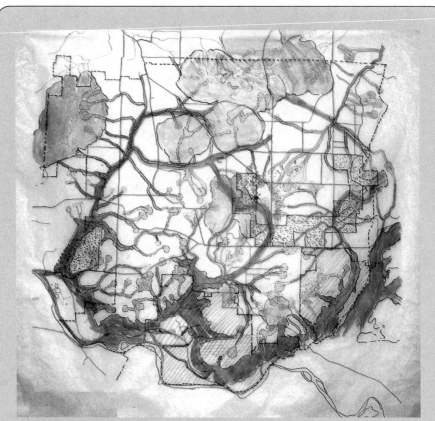

Sketch of the natural features synthesis map. The map shows extensive stream systems and associated riparian corridors. Upland buttes, forest blocks, and class 1 soils for farming are also shown.

Client goal:

The clients had generally taken positions against urban growth boundary (UGB) expansions. In this case, they decided to see whether there were circumstances under which they could embrace an expansion. Would it be possible to open up a new area for development and avoid the negative social, ecological, and economic consequences of sprawl? Would it be possible to have a clean, green, and equitable model for urban expansion? If so, what would it look like?

Participants:

Over eighty stakeholders participated in "outer table" workshops and twenty-four stakeholders were at the design charrette "inner table." Stakeholders from the public sector came from transportation, economic development, and environmental protection agencies at state, county, and local levels. Nongovernmental organization representatives from housing, transportation, and environmental groups and private sector representatives from the development industry also participated. The charrette was facilitated by six senior-level and six staff-level design facilitators.

Political context:

The clients hoped to influence the direction of planning for the region by proposing a more sustainable model for development in advance of

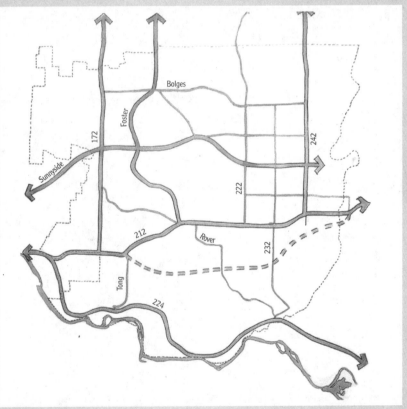

Major road diagram produced by the Go team. A new system of north/south and east/west streets eliminates the need for a proposed east/west freeway.

the Portland Metropolitan (Metro) Council's production of its own plan. The clients also wished to use the plan to clarify the rationale behind their eventual support for, or opposition to, Metro's eventual decisions on urban growth boundary expansion and its associated planning and community design framework (the Damascus Area Concept Plan).

Project goal:

The Damascus Area Design Workshop was an effort to create a regional model for this potential urban growth boundary expansion area that would be environmentally sound, that would provide a variety of housing and job choices for current and future residents, and that would fairly distribute the benefits and burdens of development among current and future residents of all incomes and backgrounds. This effort involved residents of the local area and region with a variety of interests and perspectives. Its goal was stated as follows:

> to apply design principles for urbanization that respect the unique visual quality and rural history of the area; use land efficiently; protect and restore natural areas and ecological processes important to people, fish, and wildlife; preserve clean and natural flow in area streams; improve air quality; protect and create opportunities to grow food; provide for a fair share of the region's new jobs; include ample housing, schools, public infrastructure and facilities and transportation choices in every neighborhood; and preserve and create cultural opportunities throughout the community.

This overly long and complex goal was necessary to satisfy a varied and voluble stakeholder community. It did not cripple the process and was necessary to achieve consensus, but a shorter goal would have been far better if possible.

Project principles:

This project used a set of principles established prior to this initiative by 1000 Friends of Oregon and Coalition for a Livable Future. The principles were meant to generate a model for urban development that

- uses land efficiently (in order to conserve other farm and forest lands)
- protects and restores natural areas important to threatened salmon and other fish and wildlife and preserves clean and natural flow in area streams
- protects opportunities to grow food, inside and outside the UGB expansion area
- provides for a fair share of the region's new jobs
- includes ample green spaces accessible from every neighborhood
- provides many choices among types of housing and ways to travel in every neighborhood
- preserves and creates cultural opportunities
- creates neighborhoods where families of all incomes can choose to live
- is fair in the way it distributes the regional burdens (taxes for new roads and other improvements) and benefits (e.g., jobs, parks, and schools) of growth

The results of the project were intended to be useful to local and regional residents, local governments, and Metro as they decide whether, when, and how to expand the regional UGB.

Project objectives:

The Damascus Area Design Workshop had thirty-eight objectives, which is too many. However, this charrette had an ambitious agenda that touched on the concerns of a very wide range of stakeholders. Consensus on the list of objectives could be reached only if the long list of imperatives as understood by the various stakeholders were acknowledged in the design brief. The thirty-eight objectives were organized into four categories, as shown below: transportation, community design, natural systems restoration, and economic development.

Transportation

1. Provide transportation choices for residents, including transit, bike, foot, and auto—choices for those who own a car and for those who don't.
2. Integrate land use and transportation design in order to decrease average trip length and vehicle miles traveled.

3. Ensure that job sites, schools, shopping, and recreation, have efficient connections to the new communities as well as to the rest of the region.

4. Develop an interconnected local street and pathway system that makes it easy to get around but respects the character, identity, and landscape of the Damascus area.

5. Design a regional transportation system that accommodates freight and recreational traffic and that respects the visual/aural quality and ecological integrity of the Damascus area.

6. Ensure that the transportation system is compatible with and/or strengthens local and regional economic development and other design objectives.

Community Design

7. Ensure that every neighborhood includes well-designed, energy-efficient homes for people of all income levels, meeting or exceeding Damascus area target for affordable housing. Suggest ways to ensure that those communities remain mixed-income over the long term.

8. Preserve, to the maximum extent possible, at least an equal number of housing types and tenures to those presently existing, particularly affordable homes, seeking ways to grow the new community incrementally.

9. Ensure that there is a balance of jobs to housing in the area such that sufficient housing opportunities are available to households of all income levels that have a family member working in the area.

10. Ensure that housing units at each range of cost are integrated into all neighborhoods in the area (to minimize exaggerated concentrations of poverty and wealth).

11. Create designs that lend themselves to ownership and financing strategies that will protect the affordability of the housing created for low- and moderate-income people in perpetuity, ensuring that the area will include a full range of housing choices over the long term. Suggest policy tools to ensure this.

12. Create complete communities where homes, businesses, industries, schools, public facilities, and agricultural and natural areas are designed

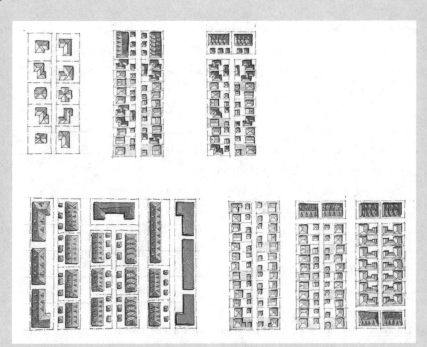

Block studies used to explore various parcel and building configurations within a uniform 600 by 300 foot block. These blocks mix various tenure types, from single-family home, to single-family home with secondary suite, to duplex, to apartment buildings.

together to magnify and reinforce community quality, identity, and value.

13. Incorporate recreation, stormwater management, and environmental and cultural education into public spaces.

14. Layer multiple public uses into community spaces and facilities (such as schools).

15. Foster local economic development and community activities that regenerate and support natural systems, strengthen the local economy, enrich neighborhood development patterns, prevent residential displacement, support the regional food system, and ensure access by all community members.

16. Identify, preserve, and celebrate local historical, cultural, and archeological heritage.

17. Provide an efficient distribution of services throughout the area.
18. Devise regionally fair and realistic funding approaches to providing and maintaining parks, schools, affordable housing, roads, and other public facilities.

Natural Systems Restoration

19. Identify and ensure that natural areas and fish and wildlife habitat are protected, restored, and enhanced.
20. Support biological diversity by protecting and restoring ecological processes and functions that sustain them.
21. Preserve, create, maintain, and link the publicly owned parks, natural areas, farmland, and open spaces that are recreational assets and natural resource treasures.
22. Preserve and restore natural stream systems to achieve clean water, natural flows, and healthy watershed function.
23. Conserve a network of natural patches and corridors, and suggest sustainable development and land management strategies for these areas that will support and enhance native fish, wildlife, and plant communities over time.
24. Provide ecological links for habitat and recreation movement both within the Damascus area and between the Damascus area and the wider region.
25. Restrict urban development on all natural hazard areas (for example, earthquake, floodplain, steep slopes, and debris flow).
26. Suggest acquisition and long-term maintenance strategies that use an integrated "systems" approach to achieve fairness among landowners.
27. Use the best available science for sustainable development; suggest strategies for environmental monitoring to advance our understanding of best sustainable development practices and adaptive management strategies for the Damascus area and elsewhere.
28. Restore urban forests in developed areas.
29. Protect important views, trees, and key cultural heritage resources.
30. Design natural areas to promote environmental education.

31. Promote taking action today to preserve opportunities to meet the above objectives now and into the future.

Economic Development

32. Ensure that plans and designs are feasible, marketable, and that public investments and amenities also lead or encourage market development of the type desired by the community.

33. Explore ways of reducing the immediate and life-cycle costs of roads and other infrastructure improvements.

34. Encourage compact growth through appropriate financing strategies, ensuring that this development pattern supports small, local business.

35. Provide the area with its fair share of living-wage jobs balanced to affordable housing stock.

36. Encourage a land ownership pattern that maximizes opportunities for small-scale and locally owned enterprise, including agriculture.

37. Ensure that a range of parcel sizes is available with sufficient transportation access to accommodate a wider range of medium and large employers and job-producing land uses such as business parks and office complexes.

38. Provide the needed infrastructure at sufficient capacities to accommodate a wide range of business types and sizes including roads, sewer, water, natural gas, power, and broadband telecommunications infrastructure.

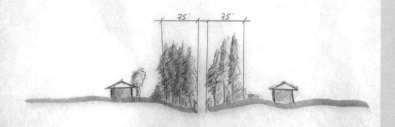

Quick study of a prototypical riparian stream corridor, part of the green infrastructure network, in relationship to backyards.

Multimodal "Green Streets" cross section. This cross section is to scale in its dimensions, but also communicates in a visual language the average person can understand.

Design principles:

For this project, partly because of the proliferation of objectives, a set of informative design principles was generated as part of the design brief. Metro did not have a robust set of community design principles; thus the project provided a unique opportunity to promulgate them. The intent was to create principles that were very clear, had powerful implications for community design, and cut across at least two of the social, ecological, and economic dimensions of sustainability.

1. Design complete communities
2. Provide an interconnected system of streets, parkways, and greenways
3. Establish green infrastructure systems to bound, protect, and reinforce all neighborhoods
4. Shift to lighter, greener, cheaper, smarter infrastructure
5. Build a healthy economy
6. Preserve present homes; introduce new ones

When comparing these design principles with the project principles above, you will note a relationship between them, but the design principles are much more physical and directed toward measurable outcomes than the project principles.

Concept plan from the Damascus Area Design Workshop that combines the green systems diagram, the movement diagram, and the 600 x 600 foot interconnectivity grid. The schematic plan produced by the Green team provided a clear framework for other more detailed plans.

Summary of numerical requirements and performance targets:

Residential density:
The density target for housing was 10 dwelling units per acre gross for all areas developed. Sixty percent of the site was left undeveloped, mostly because of topographic and hydrological constraints. The 6,000 acres of intensely developed lands yielded roughly 60,000 units of housing. Housing was to be affordable for a wide range of incomes from the wealthy to those

making 50 percent of mean average income for the region ($11,000 for one person) using purely market means. People in the latter income bracket can afford only $500 per month for rent.

Jobs:

The regional strategy for managing land use and transportation will not work if jobs and housing are not balanced. Thus the project had an aggressive jobs target with a provision to provide up to one job site per person in the area (meaning that the area would be a net importer of workers from other parts of the county).

Transportation:

The target was a 40 percent reduction in the per capita demand for auto use and a consequent shift to other modes of travel. This would be achieved through community design, density, road network configuration, and road design. Metro's livable streets program and 2040 Growth Concept plan provided a robust basis in policy for achieving this target.

Environmental:

The area is laced with salmon-bearing streams. The challenge was to add jobs and housing for over a hundred thousand people without degrading stream habitat value. Targets for low-impact development were imposed and teams were challenged to meet them.

Charrette process/choreography:

Three workshops were held prior to the charrette, focusing on the goal and objectives, on the design principles, and on the design brief. Over sixty stakeholders participated in this arduous series of workshops. The workshops were followed by a six-day charrette. Because the site was so large and the issues so difficult, the charrette was organized into issue-focused teams: the Green team focused first on ecological issues, the Go team focused first on transportation issues, and the Home team focused first on community design and jobs. Each of these teams was required to meet the objectives in the design brief, but not necessarily to design the entire huge site. Each issue focus provided a "point of departure" for design, not a sole focus. In the end, the entire site was designed in two sections, one by the Green team the other by a combined Home and Go team. The composite plan was produced by staff after the charrette.

Final illustrative plan from the Home team showing the west side of the project site with housing and jobs for 25,000 families. Media is markers on tracing paper laid over an aerial photograph. Drawing size is 4 x 6 feet.

Charrette products:

Overall site plan: 1:2,000 scale plan of entire 15,000-acre site showing all buildings necessary for 100,000 persons and 100,000 job sites.

Composite complete concept plan: Produced by staff from plans produced at the charrette.

Ecological network plan: A plan showing protected riparian stream paths, steep slopes, and important ecological resources.

Green streets and parkway sections: A plan showing the widths, transportation function, and ecological performance of street infrastructure.

Block diagrams: Plans showing the relationship between block and house configuration and affordability.

Affordability analysis: A report tied to the block diagrams analyzing costs for the market to produce housing and who could consequently afford that housing.

Transportation systems diagrams: Plans showing major and minor streets appropriate for preliminary transportation analysis.

Transportation impact analysis: A report using Metro models to prove our street network assumptions.

Industrial development analysis diagrams: Plans showing how modern industrial development could be integrated into a transit- and community-friendly network.

Final report:

The final report and the other documents listed above are accessible via the link to the project Web site given in the appendix.

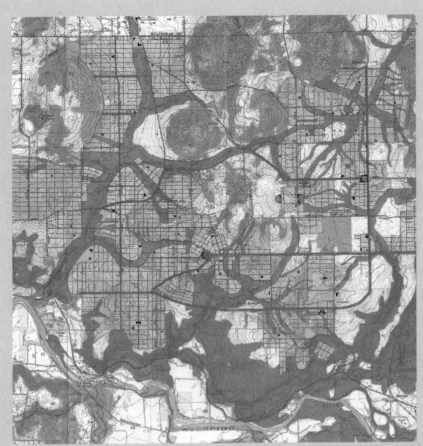

Complete depiction of the design proposal produced after the charrette in the familiar graphic format common to USGS topographic maps.

Current status:

In 2003, Metro brought the study site within the UGB, choosing this land over competing options that would have increased job distribution imbalance and consumed class A agricultural lands in Washington County. In 2004, a governance structure for the region was established, making Damascus, which was at that time an unincorporated district managed by Clackamas County, into a city.

The new city of Damascus will manage the growth of the concept plan areas. Also in 2004, Metro undertook a planning process to develop the official land use, environmental protection, and transportation design for the

Illustrative perspective of a typical Damascus area street scene conveying the desired quality of the street. Note the diversity of building types, tight setbacks, tree boulevards, wide sidewalks, and infiltration streets. All of the many high-level objectives of the charrette come together in the reality of this simple scene.

area. Most of the participants in the Damascus Area Design Workshop also had some role in this process. Although the direct causal relationship between the design workshop and the final concept plan cannot be definitively established, the final concept plan looks in most respects identical to the one generated at the workshop. More important, key strategies that emerged in the workshop—a robust system of transit and pedestrian-friendly arterials, green street systems, housing equity, riparian protection, the parkway link, and the integration of industrial lands into the fabric of the community, to name just a few—were incorporated into the final concept plan.

Plan approved by Portland Metro Council in 2005, two years after the charrette. Local road network and open space system not as complete as that shown in Damascus Design Workshop final plan, but in other ways nearly the same.

Lessons learned:
- Visioning charrettes can arm policymakers and citizens with the confidence and knowledge necessary to guide policy.
- Jurisdictional complexity adds complexity to charrette thinking. Governance must be considered when considering design.
- Visioning processes must be understood as largely political in nature. The purpose is to influence events in the "polis"; that is, to influence political events.

- Large-scale areas are manageable using design charrettes. Large areas can be designed to a high level of detail in a short time.
- Using "points of departure for design" is an effective strategy for fleshing out issues and accelerating resolution of design products.
- Very strong nongovernmental organizations (NGOs) are vital for such an ambitious charrette. It is likely that this charrette could not work as well outside of Portland, where there is a thirty-year tradition of NGO participation in regional land use issues.
- Foundation support is also crucial for this kind of charrette. Such an ambitious undertaking performed outside of normal government channels, with no guarantee that it will deliver as promised, is a tough sell. Certain foundations are willing to take this kind of risk.

Appendix:

Design Charrettes for Sustainable Communities Links Page

Link to the links.
To avoid the effort of typing in each of these links, all of the links on this page can be accessed via this one link below. Links there are arranged as you see them here.
http://www.jtc.sala.ubc.ca/projects/designcharrettesbook.htm

Project Web Sites.
Visioning Charrettes

Sustainable Urban Landscapes, The Surrey Design Charrette
http://www.jtc.sala.ubc.ca/projects/Surrey.html

Sustainable Urban Landscapes, The Brentwood Design Charrette
http://www.jtc.sala.ubc.ca/projects/Brentwood.html

The Damascus Community Design Workshop
http://www.jtc.sala.ubc.ca/Damascus/Index.htm

Implementation Charrettes

The East Clayton Sustainable Community Design Charrette
http://www.jtc.sala.ubc.ca/projects/Headwaters.html

The Squamish Smart Growth on the Ground Design Charrette
http://www.sgog.bc.ca/content.asp?contentID=135

The Maple Ridge Smart Growth on the Ground Design Charrette
http://www.sgog.bc.ca/content.asp?contentID=97

Design Briefs.
The East Clayton Sustainable Community Design Charrette: Appendix 3
http://www.jtc.sala.ubc.ca/projects/Headwaters/PDF/Appendices%201_3.pdf

The Damascus Area Design Workshop
http://www.jtc.sala.ubc.ca/Damascus/Design%20Package_finalMay16_02.pdf

The Maple Ridge Smart Growth on the Ground Design Brief
http://www.sgog.bc.ca/content.asp?contentID=123

The Squamish Smart Growth on the Ground Design Brief
http://www.sgog.bc.ca/content.asp?contentID=132

Britannia Beach Community Visioning Charrette
    Goals and Objectives
    http://www.jtc.sala.ubc.ca/britanniabeach/goals+objectives.pdf

    Design Brief
    http://www.jtc.sala.ubc.ca/britanniabeach/design_brief.html

Sample Design Principles
    Extended Design Principles from the Damascus Area Design Workshop
    http://www.jtc.sala.ubc.ca/Damascus/Principles.htm

Sample Goal and Objectives
    Goal and Objectives for Damascus Design workshop. Pages 5 - 9 on following .pdf.
    http://www.jtc.sala.ubc.ca/Damascus/Design%20Package_finalMay16_02.pdf

Technical Bulletins.
All James Taylor Chair Bulletins
    http://www.jtc.sala.ubc.ca/bulletbody.html

East Clayton Design Charrette example Technical Bulletins
    Two Alternative Development Site Standards Compared
    http://www.jtc.sala.ubc.ca/bulletins/TB_issue_02_ADSedit.pdf

Front driveway vs. rear lane designs
http://www.jtc.sala.ubc.ca/bulletins/TB_issue_07_Lot_edit.pdf

Transportation and Community Design: the Effects of Land Use, Density and Street
Pattern on Travel Behavior
http://www.jtc.sala.ubc.ca/bulletins/TB_issue_11_Transportation_edit.pdf

The Maple Ridge Design Charrette Technical Bulletins
Transportation issues
http://www.sgog.bc.ca/uplo/mr1trans.pdf

Economic development issues
http://www.sgog.bc.ca/uplo/mr6comm.pdf

Final Presentation Slide Shows.
Maple Ridge Smart Growth on the Ground
http://www.sgog.bc.ca/uplo/mr6.21.04presentation.pdf

Britannia Beach Community Vision Charrette
http://www.jtc.sala.ubc.ca/britanniabeach/results.html

Final Reports.
Damascus Community Design Workshop Final Report
http://www.jtc.sala.ubc.ca/Damascus/damascus%20final%20report.pdf

Britannia Beach Community Vision Charrette
http://www.jtc.sala.ubc.ca/britanniabeach/results.html

Maple Ridge Smart Growth on the Ground Community Vision
http://www.sgog.bc.ca/content.asp?contentID=125

Full Implementation Plan.
City of Surrey East Clayton Neighbourhood Concept Plan
http://www.jtc.sala.ubc.ca/projects/Headwaters.html

Charrette Summary "Cheat Sheets".
Southeast False Creek Design Charrette "Cheat Sheet"
http://www.jtc.sala.ubc.ca/charrettesbook/SEFC_Cheat_Sheet.pdf

Somerset County Regional Center Design Brief Summary
http://www.jtc.sala.ubc.ca/charrettesbook/RPA_Design_Brief_Summary_Sheet.pdf

Templates.
Final Charrette Presentation PowerPoint template
http://www.jtc.sala.ubc.ca/charrettesbook/Final%20charrette%20presentation_template.pdf

Team report
http://www.jtc.sala.ubc.ca/charrettesbook/Charrette_Report_Example_Template.pdf

Breakout session questionnaire example
http://www.jtc.sala.ubc.ca/charrettesbook/Breakout_session_example.pdf

Southeast False Creek Design Charrette Questionnaire for Charrette Report
http://www.jtc.sala.ubc.ca/charrettesbook/SEFC%20Question%20Template.pdf

Endnotes

Introduction

1. See James Taylor Chair in Landscape and Liveable Environments, University of British Columbia, Technical Bulletin no. 11, "Transportation and Community Design: The Effects of Land Use, Density and Street Pattern on Travel Behaviour" (December 2001), http://www.jtc.sala.ubc.ca/bulletins/TB_issue_11_Transportation_edit.pdf.

2. See "2004 National Community Preference Survey," http://www.smartgrowthamerica.org/documents/NAR-SGASurvey.pdf, one of many independent surveys sponsored by Smart Growth America on this topic.

3. See our study comparing infrastructure per dwelling unit in P. Condon and J. M. Teed (eds.), "Sustainable Urban Landscapes: Alternative Development Standards for Sustainable Communities" (James Taylor Chair in Landscape and Liveable Environments, University of British Columbia, 1998), www.jtc.sala.ubc.ca/projects/ADS.html, especially the "matrix" section for data.

4. S. Covey, *The Seven Habits of Highly Effective People* (New York: Simon and Schuster, 1989).

Chapter 1

1. World Commission on Environment and Development, *Our Common Future* (Oxford: Oxford University Press, 1987).

2. J. Lyle, *Regenerative Design for Sustainable Development* (New York: John Wiley, 1994), 8.

3. W. McDonough and M. Braungart, *Cradle to Cradle: Remaking the Way We Make Things* (New York: North Point Press, 2002).

4. Lyle, *Regenerative Design*, 25.

5. M. Comerio, "Pruitt Igoe and Other Stories," *Journal of Architectural Education* 34, no. 4 (Summer 1981): 26–31; J. Bailey, "The Case History of a Failure," *Architectural Forum*, December 1965, 25–25; O. Newman, *Defensible Space: Crime Prevention through Urban Design* (New York: Macmillan, 1972).

6. J. Jacobs, *The Death and Life of Great American Cities* (New York: Vintage, 1961).

7. E. F. Schumacher, *Small Is Beautiful: Economics As If People Mattered* (New York: Harper and Row, 1973).

8. E. F. Schumacher, *A Guide for the Perplexed* (New York: Harper and Row, 1977), 123.

9. A. Colquhoun, "Typology and Design Method," *Perspecta* 12 (1969): 71–74, available at JSTOR.

10. R. Brody, *Problem Solving: Concepts and Methods for Community Organizations* (New York: Human Sciences Press, 1982); M. Brill, S. Margulis, and E. Konar, *Using Office Design to Increase Productivity*, vol. 1 (Buffalo, NY: Workplace Design and Productivity, 1984).

Chapter 2

1. Professor Kelbaugh is a North American pioneer of the charrette methodology. His work is captured in his recent book *Common Place: Toward Neighborhood and Regional Design* (Seattle: University of Washington Press, 1997). It was for this reason that we secured his services when we began our Vancouver-based initiative in 1994. Professor Kelbaugh was our advisor for our first two major charrettes and participated in both as a team leader.

Chapter 3

1. For support for this contention, see our Technical Bulletin no. 11, "Transportation and Community Design."

2. There is much debate about how many square feet of commercial square feet should be supplied within walking distance of new homes. In most suburban new communities no commercial space is provided within walking distance of most homes. Residents therefore have to drive to "neighborhood convenience retail" facilities that are generally located a short drive from most homes, but are too far away to walk. On the other hand, an ideal sustainable community would be one where almost all of the residents' commercial needs could be met within walking distance. Obviously, the best we can do at this time in history lies between these two extremes. For the Sustainable Urban Landscapes South Newton Design Charrette in Surry we assumed that an aggressive target would be meeting 70 percent of your commercial needs within walking distance. Other needs would require a trip on transit or by car. The language we adopted is as follows:

> The minimum figure represents 70% of the 42,000 sq. ft. (3,900 sq. mtr.) per 1,000 persons commercial floor space ratio that exists in our region at this time. Since most new commercial space is now segregated into regional shopping centres, the amount of commercial space within walking distance of new dwellings is usually much lower than this figure. Given the "walking distance to services" and "access to transit" assumptions underlying this charrette, the 70% minimum figure was considered appropriate. http://www.jtc.sala.ubc.ca/projects/Surrey/surrey%20pdfs/appendices.pdf

In later charrettes we have set a lower target, asking that around 50 percent of commercial space be located within walking distance of homes. This target is a crucial one and should be debated at the pre-charrette workshops.

3. The design brief for the Damascus Area Design Workshop contains a detailed discussion of and achievable targets for job density and street interconnectivity; see http://www.sustainable-communities.agsci.ubc.ca/Damascus/Design%20Package_finalMay16_02.pdf.

4. P. Swift, D. Painter, and M. Goldstein, "Residential Street Typology and Injury Accident Frequency," originally presented at the Congress for the New Urbanism, Denver, CO, June 1997 (Longmont, Co.: Swift and Associates, 1998).

5. For the computations behind this conclusion, see James Taylor Chair in Landscape and Liveable Environments, University of British Columbia, Technical Bulletin no. 8, "The Headwaters Project—East Clayton Neighbourhood Community Plan Environmental Benefits" (January 2001), http://www.jtc.sala.ubc.ca/bulletins/TB_issue_08_Enviroben_edit.pdf.

6. The Bill and Melinda Gates Foundation has devoted significant effort to reversing the trend toward ever larger schools. More information about their Small Schools Project is available at http://www.smallschoolsproject.org/.

7. The South Newton charrette design brief contains language that could be helpful on this topic; see http://www.sustainable-communities.agsci.ubc.ca/projects/Surrey/surrey%20pdfs/appendices.pdf.

Chapter 4

1. Lao Tzu, *Tao Te Ching*, translated by David Hinton (Washington, D.C.: Counterpoint, 2000).

Chapter 6

1. For more on the value of a "frame," see G. Lakoff, *Don't Think of an Elephant* (White River Junction, VT.: Chelsea Green Publishing, 2005). This seminal little book uses U.S. politics as a case study to show that citizens seem to require a frame within which to understand information presented, and it suggests that the provision of a frame through which to view information is often more important than the information itself.

2. Design Centre for Sustainability, "Sustainability by Design: A Design Vision for a Sustainable Region of 4 Million," http://www.sxd.sala.ubc.ca/9_resources.htm; see also links at that site to the Lincoln Institute of Land Policy's "Visualizing Density" working papers and 1000 Friends of Oregon's density demonstration reports.

Chapter 7

1. In Surrey, implementation plans are called "concept plans." Confusing, of course, but the intention of this concept plan is to regulate development. It is called a "concept plan" because developers, as their work progresses, are required to produce engineering documents that are more detailed than the "concept" plan, but conform to it. As mentioned above, this is by no means the only arcane and confus-

ing local convention that charrette organizers will confront. Organizers must be humble and depend on local municipal staff to guide them through the culture of their own decision-making process.

Southeast False Creek Design Charrette Questionnaire for Charrette Report
http://www.jtc.sala.ubc.ca/charrettesbook/SEFC%20Question%20Template.pdf

Index